MW00423746

FACT, FAITH, *and* EXPERIENCE

WATCHMAN NEE

Living Stream Ministry
Anaheim, California • www.lsm.org

First Edition, June 2002.

ISBN 978-0-7363-1873-0

Published by

Living Stream Ministry
2431 W. La Palma Ave., Anaheim, CA 92801 U.S.A.
P. O. Box 2121, Anaheim, CA 92814 U.S.A.

Printed in the United States of America

11 12 13 14 15 16 / 11 10 9 8 7 6 5 4

CONTENTS

PREFACE

Throughout his life of ministry in service to the Lord, Watchman Nee demonstrated a proper balance between knowing the objective truths in the Bible and experiencing the subjective realities contained in the divine revelation. Early in his ministry, he published an article entitled "Fact, Faith, and Experience." Between 1925 and 1934, in the early years of his ministry, he released numerous messages related to these points. He spoke of divine facts, including the assurance and security of salvation and the timelessness of Christ's work on the cross, and of the role of faith in receiving these divine facts. He also provided insight and guidance into the experience and enjoyment of Christ's accomplished facts.

This book begins with the article "Fact, Faith, and Experience." Subsequent sections contain messages that relate to the topics of fact, faith, and experience. The final message, "The Two Sides of the Truth—Subjective and Objective," provides a fitting conclusion to this compilation of messages by illustrating the balance that is struck in our Christian life when objective facts contained in the Word become alive through faith and operative in our experience. These messages are simple and most suitable for new believers, but at the same time, they contain profound insights that are helpful to mature believers.

CHAPTER ONE

FACT, FAITH, AND EXPERIENCE

In the present age of grace, everything is "by grace" (Eph. 2:8). Everything being by grace means that everything is done by God. Man does not have to do anything to be saved because "to the one who works, his wages are not accounted according to grace, but according to what is due" (Rom. 4:4). Because God deals with man according to grace, there are certain facts.

FACT

God has accomplished everything for man. Since everything has been accomplished, certain "facts" exist. And since they are existing "facts," man does not have to accomplish what has already been accomplished. All of God's works are complete.

However, God's grace is a righteous grace. This is why, with the "facts," there is still the need for human cooperation. What kind of cooperation is this? It is not to add anything to what He has finished, but to have man acknowledge that what God has done is real. This is faith.

FAITH

Faith is to acknowledge that what God has said and done is true. Faith is to accept the facts, that is, to acknowledge them as facts.

Faith is a "cashing in." I use the words "cashing in" in the sense of one cashing a check at the bank. Suppose someone gives you a check. That the bank has the money is a fact. For you to cash the check for money is to acknowledge the fact that the bank possesses whatever amount is written on the check. It takes faith to "cash in." With faith, one can cash in and thereby have the money to use. Now, to spend the money is the "experience." To have the money in the bank is the "fact," to cash the check is "faith," and to spend the money is "experience." In God's grace, what He has done for man are facts. But man must still experience these facts.

EXPERIENCE

To experience God's grace is to claim by faith the facts that God has accomplished for man. These facts are accomplished by God. What man needs is faith. The facts belong to God, and the experience belongs to man. Thus, faith is God's facts becoming man's experience. What the Bible shows us is simply "fact, faith, and experience."

SUMMARY

We know that the Lord Jesus is the Word become flesh. He is the consummation of all divine virtues and the grand total of all perfections. His living is God's living, for He is God Himself. Christ has accomplished salvation on the cross. All those who sincerely accept the Lord Jesus as Lord and Savior, at the moment they believe, God accepts them *as He accepted* the Lord Jesus. At that time, all the divine virtues and accomplishments of the Lord Jesus come upon the believers. In God's view and before God, they are the same as the Lord Jesus. God sees every Christian as He sees Christ. Christians possess all of Christ's work and accomplishments through their union with Him. This is the "fact" that the Christians have been given by God. This fact was accomplished by Christ for the Christians. This fact is that through the believers' union with the Lord Jesus, everything that belongs to Christ now belongs to His believers also. This is a fact that has been accomplished by God alone; the believers themselves have no share whatever in its accomplishment.

The Bible points out this fact very clearly. The writer of the book of Hebrews uses a particularly simple illustration to point out God's accomplished fact for us. In 9:15-17 what the Lord Jesus has accomplished for us is illustrated by a person's making of a will. A will is a promise of "inheritance" to those who receive the will. But before the one who makes the will dies, the will is not effective. Once the person dies, the recipients of the will can receive the inheritance left by the one who made the will. The Lord Jesus is the One who made the will. He has died. Hence, all that He has promised goes immediately under our name. This is the fact that we have received from Him. Although we may not take possession of the inheritance all at once or enjoy the benefit and sustenance from the inheritance, yet the inheritance *is* indeed ours; it *belongs* to us and *is* under our name already. This is an immovable fact. To *have* the inheritance is one thing; to *enjoy* the inheritance is another. The ownership of the inheritance is the "fact," and the enjoyment of the inheritance is the "experience." We have the fact of owning the inheritance, not because of ourselves, but because of the One who has left the will. The possession of the fact comes first. The enjoyment comes afterward.

The teaching of this illustration is very simple. The Lord Jesus has died and has given to us all His righteousnesses, divine virtues, perfections, victories, beauties, and so forth. By these we become the same as He is before God, and God accepts us in the same way that He accepts the Lord. This is what He has given to us. These things are *facts* from the moment we become Christians. As far as the fact goes, we are already as perfect as the Lord Jesus. But as far as experience goes, we may not be this way. The meaning of this "fact" is none other than the grace that God has given to us and accomplished for us through the Lord Jesus. This grace has been given to us through our union with the Son of God. It is possible for us to have the fact of *inheriting* the inheritance without having the experience of *enjoying* the inheritance. There is a big difference between fact and experience. Many believers are very rich in fact because everything that is God's is theirs. However, in experience they are the poorest because they do not practically use and enjoy their riches. The older son in Luke 15 is a good example of this condition. *As far as the fact* goes, he was the child who was "always with me, and all that is mine is yours" (v. 31). But *as far as experience* goes, he never had "a goat that I might be merry with my friends" (v. 29). He was the son of a rich man. This was his position, a fact. Yet it was possible for him not to have enjoyed even a goat. This was his condition, his experience.

We should be very clear concerning the distinction between the fact and the experience. These two things are two different aspects. In the first case, it is what *God* has accomplished for us; it is the position that *God* has given to us. In the second case, it is what *we* practice; it is *our* enjoyment of what God has given to us. At present, believers tend to go to the extreme. Some (actually the majority) do not know the riches they have in the Lord Jesus. They do not know that everything that the Lord Jesus has accomplished *is* theirs already. They plan and scheme to secure grace. They try to work out all kinds of righteousnesses by their own strength in order to meet God's demand and satisfy the inclination of their new life. Others (not a few) think that they understand God's grace all too well. They think that the Lord Jesus has already exalted them to a matchless position. They are satisfied already and do not seek to put into practice experientially the grace that they have received from the Lord Jesus. Both kinds of people are wrong. Those who pay attention to experience and forget the facts are bound by the law. Those who pay attention to the facts and despise experience take grace as an excuse for indulgence. On the one hand, a Christian should understand through the Scriptures his lofty position in the Lord Jesus. On the other hand, he should examine under God's light whether or not his walk matches the grace of his calling.

God has placed us in a most lofty position. Through our union with the Lord Jesus, all of the Lord's accomplishments and victories are ours. This *is* our position in fact. The question now is how we can experience all of the Lord Jesus' accomplishments and victories. Between the fact and the experience, that is, before the fact can be turned into experience, before God's accomplishment can be turned into man's practice, there is still the step of faith.

This step of faith is nothing other than the "utilization" or "management" of the inheritance. The Lord has left us a will. He has died, and the will is now in effect. We should no longer hold an indifferent or unconcerned attitude. Instead we should rise up to "utilize" the inheritance that we have received so that we can enjoy, or experience, the blessing of the inheritance. We are God's children already. All that God has is now ours (1 Cor. 3:21-23). We should not be like the older son who vainly possessed the promises without entering into the enjoyment of them. Due to his foolishness and unbelief, he did not ask nor did he utilize. Hence, he did not have anything. If he would have asked to exercise his right as a son, he would have had not just one goat but thousands upon thousands of them!

What we need now is nothing other than the *utilization* by faith of what God has promised to us; we should "cash in" by faith what God has prepared for us in the Lord Jesus. For the one who is to inherit a will, there are two things he has to do before he can enjoy and experience the inheritance. First, he has to *believe* that there is an inheritance. Second, he has to rise wholeheartedly to manage this inheritance. Of course, if one does not believe that there is an inheritance, he will not rise up to manage it. Therefore, we must first *acknowledge* that God has indeed made the Lord Jesus our "wisdom...righteousness and sanctification and redemption" (1 Cor. 1:30), that all of the Lord's accomplishments and victories *are* our accomplishments and victories. If we do not have this faith, not only can we *never* expect any spiritual experiences, but we are sinning against God and doubting His work! Second, those in the world manage an inheritance with their physical strength. But for us to manage our spiritual inheritance, we have to use our spiritual strength, which is faith. As this spiritual inheritance is already ours, we must advance one step further by faith to "cash in," to utilize, and to manage our inheritance in the Lord Jesus.

In the Old Testament we see another instance which can adequately show us the relationship between fact, faith, and experience. This is the history of the Israelites entering Canaan. In the old days, God promised the land of Canaan to the Israelites. He mentioned this to Abraham, to Isaac, to Jacob, and even to the tens of thousands of people who left Egypt. To God, the land was already given. God promised to fight for them and that they would overcome all their enemies. It was a *fact* that God had given the land and the peoples of Canaan to the Israelites already. Although the fact was there, they did not yet have the experience. As far as the fact was concerned, the land was theirs already, yet in experience they still did not own an inch of it. This is why they had to "*go up* at once and possess it," for they were "well able to prevail" (Num. 13:30). However, due to their unbelief, despite the fact that God had given them the land, they were not able to possess it in experience. After one generation, God told Joshua, "Every place that the *sole of your foot* shall tread upon, that have I given unto you, as I said unto Moses" (Josh. 1:3). They were to inherit the land that God had given them with the soles of their feet. Later when they went up, they inherited the land.

This shows us the secret of substantiating the perfection of Christ. God has already given us what Christ "is," "has," and "has done"; they are all ours already. Now what we have to do is to experience all that He is, has, and has done. There is no other way to experience all this except to acknowledge that Canaan is good; if we will realize every inch of God's land with the soles of our feet, we will indeed find ourselves inheriting the land that God has given to us. God gives; we believe and receive. This is fact, faith, and experience.

DEFINITIONS

Fact

Facts are God's promises, His redemption, His works, and His free gifts.

Faith

Faith denotes the way man believes in God, trusts in His work and redemption, and claims His promises. It is a kind of working and attitude through which God's facts are transformed into man's experience.

Experience

Experience is the proper living of the believers, which they secure through believing in God. It is the expression of the life of Christ practiced in the believers' living. Experience is the realization of all Christ's accomplishments and victories.

It is the practical application, manifestation, and living out of God's facts. The histories of all the saints recorded in the Bible belong to this category.

Not only those who are teachers but all believers should know the interrelationship of these three: fact, faith, and experience. Otherwise, they will be confused in their living and in their teachings. Furthermore, they will find many contradictions and apparent disagreements in their reading of the Bible.

I am afraid that up to this point I have still not presented the scriptural teachings in a clear way. For this reason, I want to present a few great doctrines in the Bible as proofs.

We Christians have believed in the substitutional death of the Lord Jesus and have experienced the effect of His redemption. Redemption is an experience for the *sinners;* we *Christians* have already been redeemed. For us, redemption is a past experience. It seems as if we have no need to speak of it anymore. Yet for the sake of illustrating the relationship between these three things—fact, faith, and experience—and in order to show us their continuity and importance, I will first use as an example an experience that we have already had.

REDEMPTION

Redemption is a very great doctrine. It is something that we should understand. The redemption of our Lord Jesus is for the whole world. We have the following verses to prove this point:

The Lamb of God, who takes away the sin of the *world!* (John 1:29).

For God so loved the *world* that He gave His only begotten Son (John 3:16).

He Himself is the propitiation...for those of the whole *world* (1 John 2:2).

Who gave Himself as a ransom for *all* (1 Tim. 2:6).

The Savior of *all men* (1 Tim. 4:10).

After reading these verses, we can see that the redemption of Jesus is for the whole world. Hence, it is possible for everyone in the world to be saved. The Lord's redemption is an accomplished fact.

However, the Bible tells us that *not everyone* in the world is saved. If a man does not understand the teaching concerning "faith," he may think that whether or not a man believes in the Lord's vicarious death, he is saved anyway. It seems to him that since Jesus has died for the whole world, the whole world need not die anymore, and there is no need to be concerned if one believes or not. This may seem very reasonable, but actually it is very unreasonable, for this would absolve sinners of all their responsibilities. If this were the case, there would no longer be the need for believers to preach the gospel.

Although the Bible says that Christ has died for the world, it also says that those who believe will be saved. The following Scriptures testify to this:

That every one who *believes*... (John 3:15).

He who *believes* into Him...; he who does not *believe*... (John 3:18).

Believe on the Lord Jesus (Acts 16:31).

Through the *faith* of Jesus Christ to all those who believe (Rom. 3:22).

Him who is of the *faith* of Jesus (Rom. 3:26).

Your sins have been forgiven you because of His name (1 John 2:12).

We can quote many more Scriptures, but the above verses are sufficient to prove that a man has to believe. This means that although Christ has died for the world, the world must still apply His death and reckon it their own death. Otherwise, the death of Christ will have nothing to do with them. Although the Scripture says, "For God so loved the world that He gave His only begotten Son," the Bible does not stop here. Following this it says, "That every one who *believes* into Him would not perish, but would have eternal life." First Timothy 4:10 says, "The living God, who is the Savior of all men." God sent His Son into the world to die for men. Hence, He is able to be the Savior of all men. He is the "Savior..., especially of those who *believe*." These are the ones who have believed.

After believing, there must be the experience. If one

believes in God's fact, there surely must be the experience of the fact. Please consider the following Scriptures:

He who believes into Him *is not condemned;* but he who does not believe *has been condemned already* (John 3:18).

He who...believes...*has eternal life* (John 5:24).

Every one who believes into Him *would not perish, but would have eternal life* (John 3:16).

Justified out of faith (Rom. 5:1).

Hence, when man believes that the salvation God has prepared for him is a fact, and when he applies this salvation, he is saved.

DYING WITH THE LORD

Let us now explain the matter of fact, faith, and experience in relation to our dying with the Lord. It is just as important for believers to know the matter of dying with the Lord as it is for sinners to know the matter of redemption.

Fact: When Christ died on the cross, not only did He die for the sinners, but the sinners *died in Him* as well. He not only died for sins, but He brought death to the sinners as well. It is a fact in God that the sinners have died with Jesus on the cross. The following Scriptures prove this:

One died for all, therefore *all died* (2 Cor. 5:14).

Knowing this, that our old man has been *crucified with Him* (Rom. 6:6).

We who have *died* to sin (Rom. 6:2).

After seeing these few verses, we can realize that in God's view the believers have been crucified with Christ on the cross already. When a believer is not aware of this fact, he will try to crucify himself day after day and will find that no matter how much he tries, he does not die. Little does he realize that we are dead in Christ already. We should not try to crucify ourselves; rather, we should apply His death by *faith* and reckon His death as our death. Baptism is the demonstration and acknowledgment of faith. It both demonstrates and acknowledges the fact. Romans 6:3 says, "Baptized into His death." "Baptism into His death" (v. 4) is the demonstration and acknowledgment of our application through faith of this death.

We are dead, we have been crucified with Him, and our death and our crucifixion with Him are facts, yet the Word of God goes on to charge us to "reckon [ourselves] to be dead to sin" (Rom. 6:11). Reckoning is an act of faith. We do not consider ourselves dead, because we cannot consider ourselves dead. We may try to consider ourselves dead day and night, but how can one actually consider himself dead? The more we consider in this way, the more we will realize that we are alive and that we are capable of and even prone to sinning. The only way is for us to "reckon" ourselves dead in Christ. Christ's death is our death. If we have this faith, we will have the *experience* of dying with the Lord. In the Bible, Paul is a good pattern of a person who had the experience of dying with the Lord. He said, "The cross...through whom the world has been crucified to me and I to the world" (Gal. 6:14). He also said, "To know...the fellowship of His sufferings, being conformed to His death" (Phil. 3:10). Again he said, "I am crucified with Christ" (Gal. 2:20). If a believer is to have the experience—the life experience—of dying with the Lord, he cannot do so by his own methods. He must take God's way, the way of fact, faith, and experience.

It is a fact that the believers have been crucified with Christ on the cross. Do you believe this fact? Are you willing to accept this fact and to reckon yourselves dead? If you believe, you will have the same experience of dying with the Lord that Paul had.

All of the teachings in the Bible concerning God's way of dealing with man follow the order of three things: fact, faith, and experience. All that God has done is perfect. The way He deals with the world is to accomplish all the works on behalf of the world, so that they will not need to use any human ways, but rather, receive and claim by faith alone. Since God deals with man in grace at present, He does not need any work from man (Rom. 4:4). The same principle applies to crucial doctrines such as "sanctification" and "victory."

SANCTIFICATION

Sanctification is not a work of our own. Sanctification is accomplished for us by God. The Bible says, "That He might sanctify the people through His own blood" (Heb. 13:12). "For by one offering He has perfected forever those who are being sanctified" (10:14). Sanctification is an accomplished fact. Since Jesus has died, we are all sanctified. Nevertheless, 1 Peter 1:16 charges us to be "holy." Why does it charge us in this way? The reason is that though believers are sanctified, this sanctification is merely a fact with God; it is not yet an experience in the believers' lives. In order for one to be sanctified, he has to apply the sanctification accomplished through the death of Jesus, taking this as his sanctification. Only then will he live a sanctified life.

VICTORY OVER THE WORLD

Concerning victory over the world, the same thing applies. First, there is the accomplished work of Christ, which is God's fact. Jesus says, "I have overcome the world" (John 16:33). Second, there is our faith, for "the victory which has overcome the world [is] our faith" (1 John 5:4). When a man claims the victory of Christ as his victory, he overcomes the world. This is an experience in life that comes after we have believed. Facts are works of God; faith is our trust in God's works; while experience is the spiritual encounters in our life. Not only does sanctification follow this principle; many other major doctrines concerning God's way with man also follow this principle.

All of God's facts are God's own works; they do not come from man's struggle. God's facts, such as sanctification and victory, cannot be accomplished by the believers' prayer, work, self-denial, holiness, charitable donations, or planning. God's facts are accomplished by God alone. God has entrusted all His enterprises to *Christ*. Only by faith can we appropriate these facts; there is no other way.

Let us now consider an example to see the great difference between God's fact and man's experience. According to God's fact, the church in Corinth was sanctified in Christ (1 Cor. 1:2). It was the temple of the Holy Spirit (6:19). It had been washed (v. 11). Yet in experience, it was "altogether a defeat" for them, for they wronged and defrauded (vv. 7-8) and sinned against Christ (8:12). The reason for this is that they did not apply the grace (i.e., the fact) that God had prepared for them. The result was a loss. The high position that we have obtained in fact does not come through our self-effort, diligence, self-buffeting, or pretense. We do not obtain this practical experience by exerting our own effort. In order to experience the reality of the fact that God has prepared for us, all we need to do is exercise our faith to claim what the Lord has accomplished for us and to count it as our own. The perfect and *genuine* faith is that which daily *acknowledges* the works (i.e., facts) that the Lord has accomplished. The meaning of claiming is to acknowledge daily all that the Lord has accomplished for us, that is, to acknowledge that all these accomplishments are effective in us. Then, when temptation comes, we will *live out* these accomplishments *as if* we have *already* attained to the position (the fact) that the Lord has placed us in. If we do this, our experience will follow.

A believer who is high in spiritual achievement is not high in himself. Rather, it is his claiming that makes him high. The spiritual experiences of the believers are not isolated matters. This means that there is a basis to these experiences; they do not exist in themselves or evolve around themselves. The experience of the believers' spiritual life is fully based on the facts that God has accomplished for them. The facts are the basis, the experience is the accomplishment, and faith is the process. In other words, the facts are the cause, faith is the way, and experience is the result. The experience of the believers' spiritual life is just the end result, the final achievement. Before there can be any lofty spiritual life in the believers, there first must be the perfect work of the Lord Jesus as its wellspring. It is absolutely impossible for a believer to try to be sanctified, to overcome, or to die by his own effort. Sanctification, victory, death, and so forth do not come from self-effort. They come from: (1) acknowledging our sanctification, victory, and death to the self in the Lord Jesus Christ, and (2) practicing it by believing that one is joined to the Lord Jesus in life and that one *will be* as sanctified, victorious, and dead to the self as the Lord Jesus is. The Lord Jesus has already encountered every experience that we have and will have. To claim by faith is to reckon as ours all that the Lord Jesus has and to *apply* through an attitude and a conduct of faith all that we have counted as grace.

Here we must never forget the Holy Spirit. Why does God's fact become man's experience through his faith? It is because of the work of the Holy Spirit. When we believe in God's facts shown in the Bible and when we claim these facts, the Holy Spirit will apply to us all the graces that God has accomplished for us in Christ, making them real to us in our lives. In this way, they become our personal experiences. An acknowledging and claiming faith opens the door for the Holy Spirit to work and to apply in our lives all that the Lord Jesus has accomplished so that we will have the practical experience. The work of the Holy Spirit is based upon the facts of God. The Holy Spirit does not accomplish any fact for us; He only makes the things that have been accomplished real and living in our lives. God has accomplished all the facts in Christ. What we must do is acknowledge and claim these facts, trusting in the Holy Spirit to apply in our lives what God has accomplished so that we will have the spiritual experiences.

SECTION ONE

FACT

CHAPTER TWO

ASSURANCE OF SALVATION

Every time I go to a place to preach God's gospel of grace, I always ask the local Christians one question. I believe all those who can answer me with a clear "yes" are joyfully enjoying the grace of God. The question is, "Are you already saved?" In other words, do you really know that you are saved? Among a thousand people, one can only find two or three who know that they are saved. Sometimes, among a whole congregation, one cannot find one person who knows that he is saved. Then I ask these ones, "You have received the Lord Jesus and have accepted Him as your personal Savior. You have trusted in the blood of His cross to wash away your sins. Why do you still not know that you are saved? If a man falls into the water, and another man pulls him out, after the first man comes to his senses, he will surely know whether he is still in the water or safe on the shore. You should know whether you are a perishing man or a saved man who has obtained God's grace." Many people would not respond clearly with words, but their answer always seems to be, "I do not know if I have been saved. How can I say that I am saved while I am still living on earth?"

I think many of the readers of this message would answer this way! This is exactly where our mistake lies. Our belief in the Lord Jesus is not like gambling, winning when we are lucky and losing when we are not lucky. The salvation that comes through believing in the cross of the Lord Jesus is fully guaranteed. We do not have to wait until we die before we can know if we are saved or not. We can know this now. This is the clear teaching of the Bible. Please read a few verses:

"Therefore let it be known to you, men, brothers, that

through this One forgiveness of sins is announced to you; and from all the things from which you were not able to be justified by the law of Moses, in this One everyone who believes is justified" (Acts 13:38-39).

We cannot obtain justification by God through our own work. We have many sins, which make our heart sad whenever we think about them and cause us to think that we are not saved. But although we can fail, the Lord Jesus is still trustworthy. If we believe in Him, our sins will be forgiven. All those who believe in Him will be justified. How great is the Lord's salvation! God's Word says, "Let it be known to you." We should know what? We should know that once we have believed in the Lord Jesus, our sins are forgiven, and we are justified. You are saved! When God says, "Let it be known to you," we can know if we are saved or not. We should not refuse Him. We should commit our sins to the Savior and believe in His accomplished salvation for us. We will then be saved.

"This is the testimony of God that He has testified concerning His Son. He who believes into the Son of God has the testimony in himself; he who does not believe God has made Him a liar because he has not believed in the testimony which God has testified concerning His Son. And this is the testimony, that God gave to us eternal life and this life is in His Son. He who has the Son has the life; he who does not have the Son of God does not have the life. I have written these things to you that you may know that you have eternal life, to you who believe into the name of the Son of God" (1 John 5:9-13).

He who has the Lord Jesus has life. He who does not have Him does not have life. Have you accepted the Lord Jesus as your Savior? If you have, you have life already, and you are saved. The Lord Jesus said Himself: "He who believes has eternal life" (John 6:47). God has testified for His Son that He has given to us eternal life. This passage of the Scripture says that if we do not believe in the testimony that we have eternal life, then we are making God a liar. God says all those who have trusted and accepted the Lord Jesus have eternal life. Would God lie? We should believe that we who have been washed by His blood are saved already. God said, through the apostle John, that He wrote these words that we may know that we are saved.

The testimony of the Bible is that we can know if we are saved. This is not something that happens only after we die; we do not have to wait until the coming age before we know. While we are living on earth today, we should know if we are saved or not. If we are not, we should make haste to believe in Jesus Christ and come to God through trusting in His saving accomplishment for us. If we are saved, we should give much thanks to God's grace and should live on earth like saved persons. "Behold, now is the well-acceptable time; behold, now is the day of salvation" (2 Cor. 6:2). God accepts us now and saves us now, rather than after we die.

Sometimes, when I ask a person if he is saved, he answers, "I am only trying my best to do good and to serve God, hoping that I can eventually be saved." Alas, this is also wrong. This means that he does not understand the way of salvation. Do you think that you can be saved in the future by trying your best to do good and to serve God? We have to know that none of our merits and works are acceptable before God. "All our righteousnesses are like a soiled garment" (Isa. 64:6). Do you think that merit and work will save you? No, ten thousand times no! The Bible clearly says, "You have been saved...not of yourselves; it is the gift of God; not of works that no one should boast" (Eph. 2:8-9). Salvation comes through trusting in the Lord Jesus, "who Himself bore up our sins in His body on the tree" (1 Pet. 2:24), "the Righteous on behalf of the unrighteous, that He might bring you to God" (3:18). He has accomplished the work of salvation. All you have to do is to believe and obey Him. "Believe on the Lord Jesus, and you shall be saved" (Acts 16:31). Do not try to be saved by your own work. No matter how good your works are, they cannot save you, for "you have been saved...not of works" (Eph. 2:8-9). If you trust in the accomplishment of the substitutional death of the Lord Jesus on the cross, you will be saved. If you do not accept the Lord Jesus as the Savior, there will be no hope for your salvation because you cannot save yourself. If you accept the Lord Jesus as the sin offering, you do not have to hope to be saved because you have eternal life already.

We only hope for things that we have not yet obtained. If we have them already, we do not need to hope for them anymore. When a child's father leaves his home, the child hopes very much to see the father. But when the father returns home, the child is extremely glad. If the mother asks the child, "Do you still hope to see your father?", the child will answer, "I have seen my father already. Why do I still have to hope to see him?" Indeed, if we have obtained something already, we do not need to hope for it anymore. Either the world believes in Jesus and is saved and has eternal life, or it is not saved and is perishing. There is no middle ground between the two things. "Every one who believes into Him...[has] eternal life....he who does not believe has been condemned already" (John 3:16-18). The Bible divides humanity into two classes: those who are saved and those who are perishing. There is not a third class of those who hope to be saved. If you have indeed believed in Jesus Christ as your Savior and have believed in His death on the cross where He bore your sins for you, you are saved already. You do not have to hope to be saved anymore. If some would ask a man who has been rescued out of the water, "What do you want?", would he say, "I hope to get on shore"? Is such an answer sensible? Brothers, if you have believed in the Lord Jesus, you have eternal life already. Why are you still doubting? You have received it already. Why still hope for it? Simply praise the Lord instead!

There are others, when I ask about the question of salvation, that answer, "While I live on earth today, I indeed trust in the accomplished work of the redemption of the Lord Jesus. But I dare not say whether I am saved or not. I have to wait until I die and go before the Father to be judged as either a goat or a sheep. If He says that I am a sheep, then I will be saved and be most happy. If He says that I am a goat, then I will perish and go to hell in misery."

Alas, is this future not a pitiful one? Speaking truthfully, if I did not know that I was saved, I would be afraid that I would be unable to take my meal today; and I would not be able to sleep tonight. Thank the Father, for He has accepted us and has given us the eternal life! Do you really believe in the merit of the Lord Jesus' redemption? If we have believed in Him, do we have to wait until we die before we know whether we are saved or perishing? Please look at the word of the Bible. The Lord's own words are the most trustworthy of all.

"For God so loved the world that He gave His only begotten Son, that every one who believes into Him would not perish, but would have eternal life" (John 3:16). Is not this verse very clear? "For God so loved the world that He gave His only begotten Son." This is what God has done. He has loved, and He has given. He has given the Lord Jesus to the world, to die for the world and accomplish salvation on the cross, so that everyone who believes in the Lord Jesus would have eternal life and not perish. If you have believed in the Lord Jesus, you have eternal life already and will no longer perish. John 3:16 is the most recited verse. But unfortunately, many people are not familiar with John 3:16 after all. John 3:16 clearly says that as soon as you believe in the Lord Jesus, you do not perish, but have eternal life. But many believers change John 3:16! If they have believed in the Lord as their Savior but consider that they are not yet saved, they change John 3:16! They change it without knowing about it! They change John 3:16 to something like this:

"For God so loved the world that He gave His only begotten Son, that every one who believes into Him will perhaps not perish, and perhaps have eternal life after a month, two months, a year, ten years, a few decades, or after they die."

Thank God that the Bible is not written this way. The Bible has not put those words there. The Bible links "every one who believes into Him" with "would not perish, but would have eternal life." Whenever we believe in the Lord Jesus and have our sins washed by the blood; at that moment, we do not perish, but have eternal life. "Every one who believes into Him...would have eternal life" (John 3:16), without waiting until they die to have it.

The parable of the goats and the sheep has been misinterpreted by the church throughout the centuries. It has been applied to the believers. The word "nations" in Matthew 25:32

refers to the Gentiles. God has divided the world into Jews, Greeks, and the church of God (1 Cor. 10:32). The church has nothing to do with the Gentiles anymore. The judgment of the goats and the sheep refers to the judgment of the Gentile nations at the coming of the Lord Jesus with His saints. We the believers will not be judged there.

Those who have believed in the Lord Jesus will not be judged with respect to salvation and perdition. The Lord Jesus' crucifixion on the cross has borne the judgment of their sins for them. He has taken the punishment of their sins. He has solved the problem of sin for them. Those who have believed in Him have accepted Him as their substitute. He has been judged and has died for them. Of course, they do not need to be judged or to die anymore. "There is now then no condemnation to those who are in Christ Jesus" (Rom. 8:1). Please read again the words of John 5:24. "Truly, truly, I say to you, he who hears My word and believes Him who sent Me has eternal life, and does not come into judgment but has passed out of death into life."

How sweet are the Lord's words! No one can speak like Him! These clear words are like music to a sinner's ears. Since He said "truly, truly," can they be untrue? Surely they cannot be. The Lord Jesus says that the one who hears and believes "has eternal life." This is a "truly, truly" saying. He says that such a one "does not come into judgment." This, of course, must be "truly, truly" also. He also says that such a one "has passed out of death into life." This also must be "truly, truly." When He says that such a one "has passed," it surely means that it "has passed." When do we use the words "has passed" in our daily life? Does not "has passed" mean that something has already been accomplished and is over? The Lord says that a person who has believed in Him "has passed out of death into life." Why do we say that we have to wait until we die before we can know that we are saved? Brothers, those who have believed in Him have already passed from death into life even in this age. This is truly the gospel! Truly, truly I say unto you, a person who has believed "has passed out of death into life." He who does not believe "has been condemned already" (John 3:18). Both times that the word "has" is used in John 5:24 and 3:18, it refers to something that is decided now.

Perhaps when you read up to this point, you will think like many other believers, "Would it not be too proud of me to say that I am already saved? I am not better in any way in my conduct than others. How can I say this?"

Dear readers, for us to know that we are saved is not to be proud. The words "to be saved" are in the passive voice; they show that we are being acted upon. What is there for us to be proud of? To say that we do not need to be saved or that we have no need of salvation is indeed proud; it is indeed to consider ourselves better than others. But to say that we are saved indicates that we were sinners and were to perish, but that we are now *saved by Him* through trusting in Him. This shows how deep the Lord's grace is to us and how great is the saving work of the Lord. It shows how great the Lord's power is. It is not an exaltation of ourselves. If we know that we have received grace and are saved, of course, we will all the more praise the Lord. To sing of the Lord Jesus in our songs all the time is an exaltation of the Lord; it is not a self-boasting. The more we see the depth of our sins and the immensity of the Lord's forgiveness, the more we will love the Lord. We should say as Paul said: "By the grace of God I am what I am" (1 Cor. 15:10).

God says that we have eternal life already—that we are saved. Therefore, for me to say that I am saved is not boasting; it is to believe and to acknowledge that God is right. God is pleased when we believe in His Word. We must believe in God's Word.

It is true that our works are no better than others. But we are not saved because of our good works. The Lord Jesus did not come to save the righteous but the sinners. "For the Son of Man has come to seek and to save that which is lost" (Luke 19:10). "Christ Jesus came into the world to save sinners" (1 Tim. 1:15). Paul said that he was the foremost of all sinners, but that he had obtained mercy. If it is up to us, we will not be able to say that we are saved. Even the world cannot find one who can say that he is saved. If salvation is due to our merits and excellence, there will be no possibility for us to be saved. Those who trust in their works are shaky all the time. Sometimes their conduct is better, and they will hope that they can be saved. Sometimes their conduct is not as good, and they think that they will perish. These ones have never fully trusted in Christ. Dear readers, we are not saved because of our good works. We are saved because Christ has saved us. How great is His grace!

Many say: "I know that if one trusts in the accomplishment of the Lord Jesus on the cross, he is saved. But I *do not feel anything*. Am I saved just like this?"

Brothers! The Bible does not say: "I *give these happy feelings* to you that you may *know* that you have eternal life, to you who believe in the name of the Son of God." If the Bible were written in this way, one would not be saved if he did not feel anything. But the Bible says, "I *have written these things* to you that you may know that you have eternal life" (1 John 5:13).

"These things." What are these things? They are the words of the Bible, the Word of the Father. We know that we have eternal life and are saved, not by the way we feel, but by what the Word of God says. The Bible says that we who have believed in the Lord are saved. We are, therefore, saved. When God says that we are saved, surely we are saved, whether we feel that we are saved or not. We have believed in the Lord Jesus and have been washed of our sins by His blood. Therefore, we are saved because God's Word says so.

For example, a poor man may be very poor and cannot make ends meet; he may be living in extreme sufferings. He decides to write a letter to one of his friends, who is quite well off, to ask for help. After a few days, he does not receive any reply. He may think that his friend despises him and is not willing to help him, and his heart is in distress. The more he thinks about it, the more it seems unlikely that his friend will help him. He decides then to tell this matter to his neighbors. Some say that a friend should always help one in financial difficulties and has no reason to refuse to help. Others say that this may not necessarily be true because it is a compassionless age. When the man hears the hopeful words, he rejoices, and when he hears the discouraging words, he is in distress. The next day his friend sends someone to give him a reply. When he opens the letter, his heart jumps within him; he does not know if a promise is within. After he opens the letter, he shouts to his family, "The matter is now settled. He has written a letter to me saying that, from now on, he will take up all my expenses. All right. The matter is decided. I do not care if *others* think that it is hopeful or hopeless any longer. He has said himself that he will bear all the responsibilities. I can live now in peace."

Are not many believers like this poor man? What a pity that many children of God listen to others' talk and to their own feeling; they are drifting back and forth. The poor man was assured once he had a word from his friend. The children of God are likewise assured when they have the Word of God. God says that if we believe in Jesus Christ, we shall be saved. He has said it Himself, and everything is settled. What more is there to worry about? What are our feelings worth? What are man's ideas worth? If God says that we are saved, it is enough. His Word is the final verdict. Since God has graciously declared His faithfulness, we should accept His Word without doubt.

Some may say, "What was said may be true. But I am afraid that my faith is not perfect, and therefore, I cannot be saved."

The Bible only makes a distinction between "believing" and "not believing." The Bible does not know what an incomplete faith means. We should know that there is no merit in our believing in the Lord Jesus. God does not save us because we have attained the merit of believing. This cannot be farther from the truth! To believe is to receive (John 1:12). John 3:16 says that God "*gave*" us His Son. When we "receive" Him, everything is done. One gives and the other receives. There is no merit of the sinner involved. Salvation is fully accomplished by the Lord Jesus.

Who among us is not a sinner? We were dead in trespasses and sins. How pitiful we were! The Holy Spirit came and caused us to realize our sins. How terrible is the punishment for sin! One cannot help but tremble at the thought of the future. It is all the more pitiful when we realize that there is no way for us to save ourselves. We were wallowing in the mud and yet had no way to rescue ourselves! What an unspeakable deprivation! Thank and praise the slaughtered Lamb! He came and died for us on the cross. He stood on the ground of us the sinners. He loved us and gave Himself for us. While we were yet sinners, He died for us. He accomplished the salvation. When He died, He proclaimed, "It is finished!" (John 19:30). How precious is this word! O Lord! I can never thank You enough for Your great grace! To believe in the Lord Jesus means nothing other than a *willingness* on the part of us, the helpless and destitute sinners, to be saved by Him. He came to save, and when we are willing to be saved, the matter is settled. There is no question of complete or incomplete faith.

He says Himself, "Him who comes to Me I shall by no means cast out" (John 6:37). Since we have come, there is now only one question: "Has He cast me out?" Praise God, for Christ is faithful and trustworthy. There is no guile found in His mouth! He will never cast out those who come to Him. He will save all those who realize their sins and who will accept Him as their Savior. "Come to Me all who toil and are burdened, and I will give you rest" (Matt. 11:28). "If anyone thirsts, let him come to Me and drink" (John 7:37). This is the Lord's invitation.

Brothers, it is not just our faith that is saving us. Rather, it is His grace and faithfulness. God desires to save us. He will bestow grace on us. Will we not believe? What else is there to doubt? The Lord's love should fill our hearts and should drive out all drifting thoughts!

After some have understood this teaching, they may have a doubt in them: "If a man already knows that he is saved and has eternal life and is guaranteed heaven, will he not then sin at will? Will he not think that he is saved anyway and that he can, therefore, unbridle his lusts and sin at will? Will he not think that he is saved now, and that it does not matter anymore if he sins again?"

This is only a hypothesis. Many people think that if they know that they are saved, they will still want to sin. But this is only a *hypothesis*. In *reality*, something exactly opposite happens. If a man knows that he is saved, he will not want to sin anymore, and he will also bear heavenly characteristics in his thought and conduct. I can give you an illustration here. Today in China we are sending a few hundred people to study abroad every year. Most of them go to the United States. Suppose there is a father who wants to send his son to America. How should the son be dressed? Should he pay attention to the Chinese gowns and consider the latest fashion? Does he need to study Chinese etiquette and manners? Does he need to know all the things associated with the Chinese culture? Surely he does not. He is about to go to America. He does not need to know more about China, but he needs to learn the customs and fashions of the other country. He should learn to eat with a fork and knife, to shake hands, and to doff his hat. He should study in detail the tastes, likes and dislikes, and individual habits of the Americans. He should study the mind and characteristics of the Americans. When he speaks in English, he should have an American accent with it. When he walks, he should walk like the Americans walk. He should pursue after American fashion in his dress and attire. In other words, all those who are about to go to America have a natural tendency to act and move like an American. If a believer realizes that he has eternal life already, and is a citizen of heaven, he will surely learn the heavenly pattern in everything, in word, conduct, and walk. Those who do not know that they are saved will imitate the world and try to be conformed to it. Brothers, there is no danger of sinning carelessly for those who know that they are saved. On the contrary, those who know this will set their minds daily on the things which are above. This can be fully confirmed by the spiritual experiences of the believers. Just like those who are going to America try to be Americans, those who are going heavenward will surely learn to be heavenly persons.

Dear brothers! You have believed in the Lord Jesus Christ already. This is the most important thing on earth. This is also the greatest blessing in eternity for man! You should know that the Lord has saved you. What a comfort and joy it is for us to know that we are persons with eternal life in us. "Rejoice that your names are recorded in the heavens" (Luke 10:20). What a precious message! This is indeed the *glad* tidings. We can know that we are saved in this age! Formerly we were the sinners. Now we have received grace. Should we not rejoice? What gratitude and affection we have to realize that the Lord has saved us from perdition and has given us eternal life. If we know this, we will praise God all the more. We know that we cannot save ourselves. As a result, all the authority, riches, wisdom, power, honor, glory, and praise be unto the slain Lamb for now and evermore!

Now you can see how much God loves us! Since He has loved us and saved us, we should love Him out of a sense of gratitude and should live as saved persons on earth. Since He has begun the good work in our heart, He will surely complete this work until the day of Christ Jesus (Phil. 1:6). We cannot please Him by ourselves, because "those who are in the flesh cannot please God" (Rom. 8:8). We can only allow His Spirit to work in us to effect a holy living. Although sometimes we may unfortunately fail, this does not mean that we will perish again. What the Lord has given us is an *eternal* life. When we fail, we should not be discouraged. We should rise up and ask for the Lord's forgiveness. He will surely lead us on.

Once I was preaching in a place. After a brother there understood this truth, he said to me, "I did not know before that I was saved. As a result, I lived carelessly in the world. I was afraid that if I gave up everything in this life for the Lord, and then the Lord apportioned me perdition at the time of the judgment, I would as the saying goes, 'lose one's case before both the magistrate and the mandarin.' I was afraid that I would have neither the joy of this world nor the blessing of heaven! But now that I know this truth, heaven is guaranteed. Since I am a citizen of heaven already, I do not want to live foolishly in this world anymore." Indeed, if we know that our life is hid with Christ in God, we will surely set our mind on the things above. How wonderful this is! We have a wonderful Savior, and we have received a wonderful salvation. Is this not a cause for joy? Let us sing Hallelujah!

CHAPTER THREE

THE TIME OF THE CROSS—
THE TIMELESSNESS OF THE CROSS

Every time we consider the cross, it invokes wonder in us! Every time we remember the redemption of the Lord Jesus, our hearts are filled both with sorrow and with joy. To us the Lord's cross is not just a wooden cross, but a symbol of His full redemptive work and of the full salvation accomplished through this redemptive work.

When I first received the Lord, I often wondered how the men in the Old Testament, who came before the time of the Lord's crucifixion, could be saved. At that time I was a babe in the Lord and was quite perplexed by this question.

In recent years I have not seen much of the fresh power of the cross manifested in the believers. It seems that to them the Lord's death is something that happened long ago, over nineteen centuries earlier. As such, it does not seem to have any power.

I thank the Father that He has recently shown me the timelessness of the cross. Because of the above-mentioned two concepts, I consider it necessary that God's saints be acquainted with the teaching of the "timelessness" of the cross. If we realize that the cross is still extremely fresh, how much we will be touched by it!

THE LORD'S DEATH IN RELATION TO
THE OLD AND THE NEW COVENANTS

We should first read Hebrews 9:15-17: "And because of this He is the Mediator of a new covenant, so that, death having taken place for redemption of the transgressions under the first covenant, those who have been called might receive the promise of the eternal inheritance. For where there is a testament [the same word as *covenant* in the original], the death of him who made the testament must of necessity be established. For a testament [covenant] is confirmed in the case of the dead, since it never has force when he who made the testament is living." These few verses show us the relationship between the death of Christ on the cross and the old and new covenants. Under the old covenant men sinned the same way that they now do. Since there was sin, there was the need for the Savior. If a man has sinned and has not received God's forgiveness, he will have to bear his own judgment of sin. God cannot forgive man's sin simply by His mercy. To do so would put Him in unrighteousness. For this reason, in God's way of redemption He established the way of substitution. Under the old covenant He used many sacrifices and offerings to make atonement for man's sins. Since many animals died on man's behalf, man received God's righteous forgiveness. The word "atonement" in Hebrew means to "cover up." Under the old covenant the atonement was but a *covering up* of man's sins with animals' blood, because the Bible clearly says, "It is impossible for the blood of bulls and goats to take away sins" (Heb. 10:4). For this reason, at the fullness of time God sent His Son into the world to die for men. Through His one offering up of Himself, the eternal salvation of redemption was accomplished. The sins which were not removed by the blood of bulls and goats in the Old Testament are now removed through His death, for He is "the Lamb of God, who takes away the sin of the world" (John 1:29). The death of Christ marked a great change in history. His death divided the old testament age from the new testament age. Before His death, it was the Old Testament age; after His death, it is the New Testament age. The above-mentioned Scripture readings cover this point.

These three verses speak of two kinds of relationships the Lord's death has with the old and the new covenants. Hebrews 9:15 shows how He is the Mediator. Verses 16 and 17 show how He became the One who made the testament.

We have seen that everyone in the first covenant was a sinner. Although they offered to God animals as atonement for their sins, their sins were only covered; their sins were not removed. At that time God did forgive their sins because through the blood of many sacrifices God saw from a distance the blood of His Son and its effectiveness. However, unless the Lord Jesus were to die, God still could not put an end to the problem of sin in the first covenant. Sin must be removed. When Christ died, the sin under the first covenant was removed. We can see the relationship between the Lord's death and the first covenant from another angle. Every covenant has its conditions. The old covenant also had its demands. When man came short of these requirements, he sinned. The punishment of sin is death. This is why the Lord Jesus had to die on behalf of those in the first covenant and redeem them from their sins. He fulfilled all the requirements of the first covenant, terminated it, and initiated the new covenant.

Through His death He redeemed man from the sins he committed in the first covenant and became the Mediator of the new covenant. His being the Mediator of the new covenant is based on His redemption of the sins of those in the first covenant. Originally, man was to receive the promise of the eternal inheritance. However, because of his sin, man was kept from inheriting it. Now the Lord Jesus has died. Man is redeemed from sin, and the called ones are qualified to receive the eternal inheritance. Hence, the Lord Jesus became the Mediator through the death on the cross. On the one hand, He brought an end to the sins of the old covenant. On the other hand, He brought in the blessing of the new covenant. All these matters are related to His being the Mediator.

Next we should consider Him as the One who made the testament. The word "testament" is "covenant" in the original language. In the above discussion, we had the law of the covenant. All those who transgressed the law died. Christ died in order to redeem us from sin. After this we may consider the testament of the covenant. A testament means an arrangement made by a testator for the passing of his possessions to his heir at the testator's death. The Lord Jesus is the Testator, the One who made the testament. All the blessings of this age and the next belong to Him. Since He was willing to bear the sins of those in the first covenant, He is also willing to pass on all that is promised in this covenant (testament). In order to redeem man from his sins, He had to die. In order for man to inherit the testament, He also had to die. If a man is alive, the testament he makes will not come into effect. He must die before the heir can inherit the inheritance. Here we see the profound relationship between Christ's death and the old and new covenants. In short, without His death there would not be the old and the new covenants. Without His death, the Old Testament could not be complete, for the requirement of its law would not have been met. Without His death there could not be the New Testament, because there would be no way for the blessing of its testament to be passed on to the called ones. But the Lord has died. He has terminated the first covenant and has enacted the second covenant. Indeed, the New Testament was enacted by His blood.

HOW WERE MEN SAVED IN THE OLD TESTAMENT?

If the blood of bulls and goats was not able to remove sin, as we mentioned earlier, how then were those in the Old Testament saved? It was by the cross. *Man* had sinned. Hence, only *a man* could accomplish the redemption of sin. Although the animals were innocent, and although they were without blemish, they could not redeem man from his sins. Why then did God promise in Leviticus 17 that the blood of creatures was able to redeem one from sin? There must be some very profound meaning here. The things of the law "are a shadow of the things to come, but the body is of Christ" (Col. 2:17). Hence, the sacrifices and the offerings in the Old Testament all refer to Christ. Although Christ had not yet died at the time of the first covenant, God intended that all the sacrifices offered at that time be a type of Christ. Their death was taken as the death of Christ. Through the blood of many animals, God saw the blood of His beloved Son. Through many bulls and goats, He saw "the Lamb of God." Through the many sacrifices, He saw the substitutional death of Christ. When He accepted those offerings, it was as if He was accepting the merit of the death of His Son. Because of this, man was redeemed from his sins. God reckoned the innocent bulls and goats as His dear Son. Hence, He could forgive the sinners based upon the sacrifices they offered. Every time the offerings were slaughtered, they spoke of the coming sacrifice of the Son of God as the sin offering on Golgotha and of His accomplishment of the eternal work of salvation. Because the Lord is a man, He is able to redeem man from sin. Because He is God, He is able to redeem all men, past and present, from their sins.

Those who offered the sacrifices in the Old Testament, consciously or unconsciously, believed in a coming crucified Savior. All their sacrifices were to turn them to the coming Savior. Although the Lord Jesus was not yet born at that time, faith did not look at what could be seen. Rather, it looked at what could not be seen. Faith saw a vicarious Savior from afar and trusted in Him. When the time came, the Son of God came and died for men. What had only been a matter of faith then became a fact.

HOW ARE MEN SAVED IN THE NEW TESTAMENT?

We know that we are in the New Testament age. How are we saved in this age? Christ has died and salvation is accomplished. If we believe in the Lord Jesus, which means that by faith we receive Him as the Savior, we will be saved. Some have a hard time understanding how Christ could have died for them before they were even born. Indeed this presents a problem to the physical senses. Yet to faith, this is a glorious truth.

First, we must realize that time cannot restrict God. To us mortals, a few decades is a long time. But our God is an eternal God. To Him, even a thousand years do not mean much. Although time can restrict us, it cannot restrict Him. Hence, even though we believe in a Lord who died once for us many years ago, we are saved.

The Bible says that the Lord Jesus offered up Himself once and accomplished the work of redemption (Heb. 7:27). He is God. This is why He can transcend time to redeem those who were thousands of years before Him as well as those who are thousands of years after Him. Not only can He redeem those thousands of years after Him; if, unfortunately, the world goes on for millions of years more, His redemption will still be effective. Once He finished His work, it was accomplished forever. If a sinner desires to be saved now, the Lord does not need to die for him again. This one only needs to accept the merit of the Lord's one offering, and he will be saved. Our faith is not restricted by time either. Faith can lead one into the reality of eternity. As men in the Old Testament looked to a coming Savior and were saved, in the same way we look to a past Savior and are saved. The fact that the matter is past does not mean that it is over. Rather, it means that it is done. The men in the Old Testament looked forward. We at the present time look backward. Faith caused those in the Old Testament to accept a coming Savior. Will not our faith cause us to accept a past Savior?

In reading Hebrews 9:12-15 it would be very meaningful if we link together the three "eternals" in these verses. The Lord accomplished an eternal redemption. By offering up Himself to God through the eternal Spirit, we have obtained an eternal inheritance. Hence, whenever men believe in Him, they receive this redemption. We ought to realize that the worth of the cross is not determined by man. Rather, it is determined by God. God considers the redemption of the cross as eternal. Therefore, we sinners who have no righteousness of our own should acknowledge God's word as true and should act according to His word and believe in the cross of His Son and be saved.

THE TIMELESSNESS OF THE CROSS

This is the most crucial point. Although the Bible says that the Lord Jesus offered up the sacrifice for sins once, it points out that "having offered one sacrifice for sins, [He] sat down *forever*..." (Heb. 10:12). The word "one" means that the Lord's sacrifice for sins was perfect; He only needed to redeem man from sins once. However, this sacrifice for sins is *forever*. It is an eternal sacrifice for sins! This means that *not only* is the effect of this sacrifice for sins eternal, but the sacrifice itself is eternal. Although Christ has resurrected and is living forever, it seems that His cross continues to exist! May we realize the timelessness of the cross! It is not a past event of nineteen hundred years ago. It remains fresh today.

Revelation 13:8 says, "The Lamb who was slain *from the foundation of the world.*" Our Lord is the slain Lamb from the foundation of the world until now and forever. To Him, the cross is not *merely* an event of a certain time, on a certain date of a certain month of a certain year. Rather, it is something that has existed since the foundation of the world until now. When He created man, He foreknew the price of the coming redemption. He created man with His power. In the same way He redeemed man with His blood. It is as if He was crucified from the beginning when He created man. For thousands of years He suffered the prolonged suffering of the cross. The one death on Golgotha merely signified the grief God's Spirit had borne for a long time. What grace this is! What wonder this is! We have no words to express the meaning of this verse. Before the Lord Jesus left heaven, and while He was still in glory, He knew the suffering of the cross already. He knew during the thousands of years before He came. He knew this at the time of creation. Since eternity past, the cross has been in God's heart. When we consider how in eternity past God knew that He was to create man and that man would become fallen, we realize how His heart, humanly speaking, must have grieved over it. Because He so loved men, He ordained before the foundation of the world that Christ would die on our behalf (1 Pet. 1:20). Although Christ only appeared once in the last times for our sins, through His love for the world He has been grieving and aching since the foundation of the world, as if He has been crucified a thousand times already! What a pity that many people are now still grieving Him, as if crucifying Him afresh. When we realize such love of His, we cannot help but marvel and stand in awe before Him! This is God's heart! If we realize this, will we not love God all the more? Hence, humanly speaking, those in the Old Testament believed in a coming cross, while those in the New Testament believe in a past cross. Actually, there is no distinction of time and period. The cross of the Old Testament is a present one, and the cross of the

New Testament is also a present one. May the Lord open our eyes to see that the cross is timeless.

THE ETERNAL FRESHNESS OF THE CROSS

Those in the Old Testament have died. We shall, therefore, pay attention only to those in the present time. Many people push the cross back nineteen hundred years and consider it as old, outdated, and obsolete. Although it is true that world history considers Christ's Golgotha a historical event, in the believers' spiritual experience the cross of Christ is still a fresh event. It is not old, outdated, or obsolete. We can consider a few verses.

Hebrews 10:19 and 20 say, "Having therefore, brothers, boldness for entering the Holy of Holies in the blood of Jesus, which entrance He initiated for us as a new and living way through the veil, that is, His flesh." In order to understand these two verses, we have to understand the things mentioned in the Old Testament. In the ancient times, the tabernacle was divided into two sections. The first section was called the Holy Place, and the second section was called the Holy of Holies. The two sections were divided by a veil. Those entering the Holy of Holies had to pass through the veil. God's glory was manifested within the Holy of Holies. No ordinary person could enter the Holy of Holies. Only the high priest could enter it once a year. Before he entered it, he had to first offer sacrifices and make atonement for himself and the people and had to go in with the blood of bulls and goats. For us now, we enter the Holy of Holies through the blood of the Lord Jesus. This signifies the cross. Formerly, the high priest entered the Holy of Holies only once a year. Now, through the cross of the Lord Jesus we can enter the Holy of Holies any time. What is the meaning of entering the Holy of Holies? It means that we can come to God to confess our sins, fellowship with Him, and be in His presence.

Those entering the Holy of Holies had to pass through the veil. The veil signifies the body of the Lord Jesus. When He was crucified, the veil of the temple was rent in half from top to bottom. If the veil had not been rent, men could not have passed through it. If the Lord Jesus had not died and

His body not been broken, men could not pass through Him and could not enter the Holy of Holies. At the present time, we come to God through the death of the Lord Jesus. This also signifies the cross.

Our Bible tells us that this way through the veil was opened up for us by the Lord Jesus. Truly, He willingly gave up His life to redeem us.

We need to pay attention to the fact that this way is "new and living." The word "new" in the original language refers to something freshly offered or freshly sacrificed. Here we see the eternal freshness of the cross! The high priest could not rely on the offerings or sacrifices of the previous years. He had to have fresh offerings and fresh sacrifices. He only dared to enter and was able to enter the Holy of Holies through the blood of these animals. What about us now? We come to God by the blood of the Lord and through His body. Every time we come before God, we do not have to offer up sacrifices afresh. Our Sacrifice is forever fresh! The Lord Jesus' cross does not turn old with the years. Its freshness is the same today and forever as it was at the time of crucifixion. Every time we come before God, we can sense the freshness of the Lord's cross. In the ancient times, unless the high priest had fresh blood of newly offered sacrifices, he would die before the Lord. The sacrifice of previous years could not redeem him from his current year's sins. If God did not consider the Lord's redemptive sacrifice as eternally fresh, we would have perished long ago. Thank the Lord that the cross is forever fresh before the Lord. The Lord considers the crucifixion as something freshly accomplished.

This way is also "living." This word can also be translated as "forever living." This way is a way that is "freshly offered." It is also a way that is "forever living." Christ has died and has resurrected; He has accomplished salvation for us and has led us to God. We should know that Christ has resurrected and that His resurrection remains until today. We should also know that Christ has died and that His substitutional death continues until today. The greatest events in the earthly life of Christ were His death and resurrection. Both are not past, obsolete events. They are still fresh today. Since we have such a fresh, redeeming Savior, we should receive Him and come to God through Him to receive forgiveness and blessing.

Revelation 5 records how John saw the Lord Jesus Christ in heaven. He said, "And I saw in the midst of the throne and of the four living creatures and in the midst of the elders a Lamb standing as having *just* been slain" (v. 6). This is a picture of the future. When John saw the Lord in heaven, it was many years after Golgotha. Yet the Lord was like One who had *just* been slain. The words "having just been slain" can also be translated as "having been freshly slain." In heaven at the time of the ushering in of eternity, the Lord will still be the One who is freshly slain! Oh, the eternal freshness of the cross! Truly the cross passes through all ages and remains fresh! If the cross will be fresh in heaven in that day, how can we consider it as being old today? In the future when the heavenly glory breaks forth, the glory of the cross will prove unfading! When God's redeemed ascend to heaven, they will find the redemption of the cross still as fresh as before!

One point deserves our attention. In the Old Testament Christ is twice called the Lamb (Isa. 53:7; Jer. 11:19). In the Gospels and Acts He is mentioned as the Lamb three times (John 1:29, 36; Acts 8:32). In the Epistles He is mentioned as the Lamb once (1 Pet. 1:19). However, in Revelation He is mentioned as the Lamb *twenty-eight times*! The glory of the Lord's cross will outshine all ages! God purposely called His Son the Lamb in this book of eternity. The Lamb here is seen as having been freshly slain. The wound is still there! The eternal wound guarantees eternal salvation. The crucifixion of the Lamb becomes our eternal memorial. God can never forget this. The angels can never forget this, and those ascended and saved ones can never forget the redemption of the cross. Who will receive this eternal salvation? The cross is the only unshakable place. All those who have sinned should come.

THE MEMORIAL OF THE CROSS

God Himself knows the eternal worth of His Son's cross. He has manifested to all the eternal freshness of the cross of His Son. Now He desires to gain the redeemed ones so that they would know this fact also. The realization of the eternal freshness of the cross brings power. The realization of the eternal freshness of the cross brings love. The realization of the eternal freshness of the cross brings victory. The realization of the eternal freshness of the cross brings long-suffering. If we truly know the freshness of the cross, what inspiration we will receive from it! What motivation we will derive from it! If the cross is not old in our heart, we will surely have an intimate fellowship with our Lord. If a believer has forgotten the cross, it means that he has forgotten the Lord.

The Lord intends that His cross be forever fresh in our spirit and our mind. This is why He told us, "This do, as often as you drink it, unto the remembrance of Me" (1 Cor. 11:25). The words "as often as" imply "frequently." The reason the Lord established His supper is for His saints to remember Him always in His death. He foreknew that many would consider His cross as obsolete. This was why He charged His disciples to always remember His death at the Lord's supper. He knew that worldly affairs, distractions, and temptations would come and would secretly rob the freshness of the cross from us. This is why He charged us to take the supper often and to remember Him. How fresh was the cross to us when we first believed! But after many days, the cross seems to have become hazy. When we first realized the victory of the cross, how fresh it was to us! But through frequent mention of its glory, the cross seems to have become common. However, the Lord does not want to see us losing the freshness of the cross. He desires that we remember the cross often and always have the death of the Lord before us.

It is a pity that we have lost the inspiration of the cross of the Lord Jesus. The crucifixion of the Lord Jesus should be *openly portrayed before our eyes* all the time (Gal. 3:1). We must never consider the Lord's cross as a mere historical monument.

The book of Galatians is an Epistle on the cross. When the cross was openly portrayed before the Galatians, how free they were! When they tried to receive the Holy Spirit through the keeping of the law or be perfected through the work of the flesh, they lost the freshness of the cross. One can tell the spiritual condition of a saint just by his attitude toward the cross. If he considers the cross as something old, it shows that he is cut off from the source of his power.

THE CROSS AND SPIRITUALITY

What are the benefits of knowing the freshness of the cross? The benefits are innumerable. We know that anything new easily touches men. If something happened long ago, it does not have the power to stir men up. If we have the Lord's cross openly portrayed before us every day, how much we will be moved by it! Joseph in the ancient times was only willing to be Christ's disciple in secret. Nicodemus only dared come to see the Lord in the night. But when both saw the crucifixion of the Lord, they were greatly moved. As a result, they risked offending the crowd and asked for the body of the Lord for burial. The cross can make the most fearful men the most courageous ones. When they beheld Jesus on the cross and the way He suffered and was rebuked by men, the love of the cross inspired them and moved them. Hence, if we have the death of Christ before us all the time, we will be moved in the same way that they were moved. The cross will then become our strength.

"Should we continue in sin that grace may abound?" (Rom. 6:1). We should be able to answer this question. If we truly see the Lord's cross all the time, if we truly see how He suffered there, if we see the wounds on His hands and feet and the crown of thorns on His head, if we see how His love and blood mingled, and if we see His sufferings and sorrow, will we not be deeply moved, and will we not cease from doing things that do not please Him or cause Him sorrow? It is because we lack the eternal fresh revelation of the cross before us that we despise the love of the Lord.

If the cross on which the Lord died for us is forever fresh, our *crucifixion with Him* will also become unchanging. If we have a fresh revelation of the cross day by day, we will add to ourselves many fresh experiences of faith in our dying together with Him. It is because we do not see a *daily* cross that we have many experiences of *sin resurrecting* in us. If we see the eternal freshness of the cross and its ever unchanging nature, our death to sin will also be unchanging. Many children of God fail because they do not realize that the death of the cross is not just something that happened a long time ago, but something that is with us continually all the time.

We know that many times we fall unconsciously. Thank God the Father, who does not reject us because of this. The Bible says that "the blood of Jesus His Son cleanses us from every sin" (1 John 1:7). He did not cleanse us just once. The blood of His Son is still continually cleansing us. The word "cleanses" in the original has the sense of a continual action. This is the perpetual work of the cross. How wonderful it is that God has prepared for us such a salvation! If we stumble by accident, and we come to Him and confess our sins, He will forgive us, and the blood of His Son will cleanse us from all sin. What eternal freshness there is in the cross!

ETERNAL SALVATION

If we realize this, we will break forth in loud praises to God the Father. Unfortunately, many people do not know that they are saved forever. We are either not saved or saved forever. If we have once *truly* accepted the Lord's sacrifice for sin, and if we have once *truly* trusted in the merit of His cross, His cross will forever speak for us. "This is the law of the burnt offering: the burnt offering itself shall be upon the hearth on the altar *all night* until the morning, and the fire of the altar shall be kept *burning* on it" (Lev. 6:9). The burnt offering is a type of Christ, and the altar is a type of the cross. The night is a type of the present Christless age. It is the same night as the one in Romans 13:12. Since the Sun of righteousness (the Lord Jesus) departed from this world, this world has become the night. It will remain the night until He comes again. The burnt offering shall be burning until daybreak! In the present age, the merit of the Lord's redemption is continually pleading for us! In the night, the Israelites may have been in the camp still murmuring, but the burnt offering on the altar continually interceded for them! We should realize that in the same way the blood is interceding for us. Once we have accepted the cross, it speaks for us forever! This is the eternal salvation.

In the future, when we see the cross in heaven, it will not have become old through the ages. For this reason, the salvation we have received will not become a mere monument through time. Eternity will not be a monotonous and tasteless life. Eternity may be long, but it will not take away the glory of the cross. In eternity we will see God unfolding the glory of the cross for us bit by bit. Lord, teach us the eternal freshness of the cross!

For what reason do the heavenly hosts praise the Lord? "Worthy is the Lamb who has been slain to receive the power and riches and wisdom and strength and honor and glory and blessing" (Rev. 5:12). At that time we will also praise the Lord forever because of His cross. The cross is the subject of the Bible on earth today. It will be the cause of praise in glory in the future.

Brothers, how fresh is the cross! The cross does not know what time is. The cross does not know what oldness is. May we be constantly moved by it! Oh, may we be lost in the cross all the days of our life! Oh, may the cross not lose its power on us for a day! Oh, may we allow the cross to do a deeper work in us every day! May the Father open our eyes to see the mystery hidden in the cross of His Son. "But far be it from me to boast except in the cross of our Lord Jesus Christ" (Gal. 6:14).

SECTION TWO

FAITH

CHAPTER FOUR

LIVING BY FAITH (SELECTED)

"But the righteous shall have life and live by faith" (Rom. 1:17). This is the normal rule for the believers' living. We are prone to live by the excitement of the visible joys and the obvious blessings. But the Word of God says that "the righteous shall have life and live by faith." Many believers desire to have the revelation of God; they aspire to noble transformation and "third heaven" experiences. Some may encounter these at times, but the righteous must live by *faith*. The union in life that Madame Guyon experienced is seldom found in the present age. She said that her experience was such that she found it impossible for her to live apart from His life. She was able to attain to this state only through faith and self-denial.

Many believers are deeply grieved because they do not have a conscious feeling of God's presence. As a result, they cry out to God with their whole being, seeking for God as the deer seeks for a stream of water. Faith is not to touch God's presence. It is not to love Him in excitement or to express oneself in exuberance. The righteous shall live by faith—by faith alone.

Faith is like an anchor; it establishes a person. Faith is real; it is a "substantiating." Faith is also a "conviction of things not seen." Hence, it is touchable.

Those who walk by faith may have outward joy. But this is not what they are looking for; this is not their goal. A feeling of joy is merely the flowers that shine atop the dark green leaves along the path of faith.

Faith can do what nothing else can do. First, it can please God: "But without faith it is impossible to be well pleasing to Him" (Heb. 11:6). This is the life of our Lord Jesus, for

He said, "I always do the things that are pleasing to Him" (John 8:29).

Second, it bears fruit: "Who through faith overcame kingdoms, worked righteousness, obtained promises, stopped the mouths of lions, quenched the power of fire, escaped the edge of the sword, were made strong in weakness, became mighty in war, routed the armies of foreigners. Women received their dead by resurrection..." (Heb. 11:33-35). However, even though some results are obtained, one must continue to go on steadfastly by faith. He must believe in God and have faith whether *in light or in darkness*. He must fulfill his duty, moving forward to do whatever is next to do. He should advance in the way of faith even though it is an ordinary path. While he gropes in darkness and walks in darkness, he should live—*living and unceasingly working*—by faith.

If he would do this, glory will be all around him. However, those who live by faith will not see this glory themselves. Many lessons of faith are very deep and essential. Moses did not realize that his face shone, but the ones who saw this glory were blessed.

Once, a missionary returned to her country wearing a very drab dress. When a young lady there saw her dress, she felt sorry for her. The missionary turned and looked at her, but she did not say a word. However, when the young lady saw her face, she was reminded of God. That young lady never forgot that day. She was very bright and intended to study for a certain degree, but eventually, she changed her mind and became a worker of Christ. The Lord is the Victor! She is now saving many in Africa. Although that returning missionary did not see her own face, others saw it, and the Lord worked.

An unchangeable fact is that those who live by faith must look away unto the Lord Jesus. God says that we should look away unto the Lord Jesus as the Author and Perfecter of our faith. If one does this, he will reflect in word, countenance, and attitude the One he looks away to. This life is far beyond description—the righteous shall live by faith.

CHAPTER FIVE

THE SOURCE OF FAITH

Faith has a source. This source is not in the saints but in God. If the source of faith were in the saints, faith would be fragile. Who could have faith? Many children of God sadly sigh over their lack of great faith. Some lack not only great faith but even small faith. We often acknowledge that we have no faith. We wish for greater faith so that we can trust God and He can perform daily miracles for us. We wish for practical faith so that we can commit everything into the hand of God with ease and calmness. "If only we could have greater faith, everything would be fine." This is our wish. "If only we could have faith like So-and-so, then everything would be all right." This is our word of admiration. How often have we asked the Lord to increase our faith? But why do we still lack faith? Does faith only belong to a certain privileged class of saints? Is there truly no way for us to obtain greater faith? There is a way in the Lord. But only those who want faith can obtain it.

The cry of the saints today is for greater faith. But where does greater faith come from? The saints aspire to have greater faith in *themselves*. Is this a mistake? Yes, the mistake of saints is that *they* want to have greater faith in *themselves*. They seek faith from the wrong source. No wonder they never get it!

We all ask ourselves, "Do *I* have faith?" "Can *I* trust God regarding this matter?" "Is *my* faith sufficient?" The answers to these questions are always "No" and "I cannot"! What a great grief it is! We should not ask these questions. *We are not the source of faith,* so we *cannot* expect ourselves to have greater faith. The more we ask ourselves and search, seek, and look within ourselves, the more we feel we have *no* faith or very little faith! What is the reason for this? The reason is that we are not the source of faith. Since the source of faith is not within us, we cannot obtain faith if we turn within ourselves to search for it. Therefore, we must learn a lesson: we are not the source of faith. When we examine ourselves, we cannot see or feel that we have faith.

The Word of God tells us what the source of faith really is: "Faith...not of yourselves; it is the gift of God" (Eph. 2:8). This verse of the Bible is more than clear; faith is given to us by God. A similar word is found in Acts 3:16: "The faith which is through Him." Therefore, we know that the source of faith is in God, not in us. This may seem very common, ordinary, and familiar to us. But there are not many who really understand the importance of the source of our faith. If we really understood that God is the source of our faith, we would never ask ourselves, "Do *I* have enough faith? Do *I* have faith?" These questions indicate that we still do not understand that *God* is the source of our faith, because if we did, we would not ask these questions.

God is the Giver of faith; God is the source of faith. Nevertheless, the fact that God is the source of faith does not mean merely that He gives faith to us. It means that men have faith or increase in faith through God because God is the source of their faith. In other words, men have faith or increase in faith because God possesses a nature that makes it easy for men to trust in Him.

What does this mean? It means that we do not have to ask, "Do we have faith? Is our faith sufficient?" These are not the most important questions. These questions will keep us in darkness and discouragement. We should ask, "Is *God* reliable? Is *God* honest? Is *God* trustworthy? Will *God* break His promises? Are *God's* power and love real?" Because we always pay attention to ourselves, the more we search, the more we are unable to find our faith. If we pay attention to God, we will find that faith comes spontaneously. Faith does not originate in ourselves. No wonder faith cannot be found when we examine ourselves! Faith originates with God. The more we look at God, look to God, and meditate on God, the more we will have faith.

An illustration may help us understand this teaching. Once a few brothers came to talk with me about the issue of faith. They felt that they had too little faith. But I told them that it was not their faith that was too little but their *God*. If they wanted to have greater faith, they needed to have a greater God. That day I told them that faith means committing ourselves and our things to someone else. Believing in God means committing ourselves and our things to God and trusting in Him to accomplish these things for us. I asked, "When you commit your things to somebody else, do you ask, 'Do I have the faith to trust this person? Is my faith sufficient to trust him?'" You never ask these kinds of questions. Rather, you ask, "*Can* I trust him?" You do not ask, "Do I *have* faith in him?" Suppose you are an owner of a store, and you hire a manager and commit your business entirely to him. When you hired him, you *did not* ask, "Do I have faith in him? Is my faith too little? Do I have to increase my faith in him?" Instead, you asked yourself, "*Can* I trust him? Is *he* honest? Is *he* faithful? Is *he* reliable?" Since he was honest, trustworthy, and reliable, you *spontaneously* committed your entire business into his hand. You did not have to ask yourself if you had faith or if your faith was great or sufficient.

Similarly, you should trust in God. You do not have to ask, "Do I have faith? Is my faith great and sufficient? How much more should my faith be increased?" All you have to ask is, "Is *God* honest? Is *God* faithful? Is *God* reliable? Will *God* regret His promise and break His word?" If *God* is honest, faithful, and reliable, and if *He* promises and will not repent, then you do not have to search and examine yourselves to see if you have faith. You will spontaneously commit yourselves and your things to the hand of God. This is faith. Faith is not something produced from within. It is a trust that arises out of the fact that *the other party* is honest, stable, trustworthy, and reliable. Therefore, what is lacking is not greater faith but a *greater* God.

Most of the time, we do not dare commit ourselves and our things to God under the pretext that our faith is too small. Actually, the reason we do not dare commit ourselves to God is neither the absence of our faith nor the smallness of our faith. Rather, we think that God is not reliable. If God is faithful, why do we not rely on Him? If God is trustworthy, why do we not put our trust in Him? If God is reliable, why do we not depend on Him? If God will not break His word, why do we not rely on Him according to His promise? We are afraid that our God is muddle-headed, unreliable, dishonest, and always breaking His promises. This is the reason we do not have faith. Now is the time for us to confess our sins. We know a bank is honest and reliable. This is why we deposit our money in it. We ask if the *bank* is trustworthy; we do not ask if *we* have faith in the bank. When a baby is in danger, his fear ceases, and he is at peace when he just touches his father's hand or mother's face. He will not trust anyone else because they are not trustworthy to him. He trusts in his parents because they are trustworthy.

Faith is natural! It comes *spontaneously* and without reluctance because we put our trust only in those that we consider trustworthy. We do not need greater faith, we need to know the faithfulness and trustworthiness of God. If we realized that God was the source of our faith, we would no longer seek faith in ourselves. Instead, we would lift up our eyes to God and seek to know Him. When we realize that God is reliable, our faith will spontaneously grow. If we know that God is reliable, we will trust Him. If we consider God to be unreliable, we will not trust Him.

Our faith has a basis because it rests in God. We do not believe in ourselves but in God Himself. We must make a distinction: what we believe in is not *our* faith but God. The mistake of some believers is that they believe in their feelings of faith more than they believe in God. If they feel they have no faith, they do not trust in God or commit their things into God's hand. If they feel they have faith, they boldly entrust their things to God. What is this? This is not believing in God. This is believing in their own faith! We should not pay much attention to this faith. We should not ask or search to see if we have faith, and we should not trust in God only when we have faith. We should ask whether or not God is reliable. If He is—and of course He is—then why do we not trust in Him? If we think, "I am not afraid now because I have faith," then we are trusting in our own faith and not trusting in God. Likewise, if we say, "I cannot commit these things to God because I have no faith," it does not mean that we do not believe in God. This only indicates that we doubt our own faith. We fail to trust in God not because He is untrustworthy but because we do not have faith. The problem is not with God. The problem is with man. It may be true that you do not have faith, but is God unreliable? If *God* is reliable, why do you not trust in Him? You only have to be concerned about God, not yourself. If God is trustworthy, then spontaneously you will trust in Him. Otherwise, even if you have faith, it is futile. Do not trust in your own faith; your faith is not trustworthy. Instead, trust in God. "For I know *whom* I have believed"; therefore, "I *am persuaded* that He is able to guard my deposit" (2 Tim. 1:12).

The Bible not only tells us that God is the source of our faith; it also tells us that *the word of God* is the source of our faith: "So faith comes out of hearing, and hearing through the word of Christ" (Rom. 10:17). Why do I first say that God is the source of our faith and then say that the word of God is the source of our faith? Here we see the wonder of God's word. How do we know God? We know Him by the word He speaks. The word He speaks represents His heart's desire. When we understand His word, we will realize what God has promised for us and what He does and does not want to do. Only through the Word of God—the Bible—can we know God's promise. When we know His promise, we will trust in Him according to His promise and beseech Him through prayers. If we do not have the word of God, we will have nothing at all. "How then shall they call upon Him into whom they have not believed? And how shall they believe into Him of whom they have not heard?" (Rom. 10:14). If we do not have the promise of God, but mindlessly believe in Him, we will fall into a kind of superstition. Faith must be based on something. Mindlessly believing, without a basis, is superstition, and no one will receive anything from this kind of faith. If my father promises me something, I believe he will give it to me. This believing is solid because my faith is based on the promise of my father. If my father has not promised me anything, but I force myself to believe that he will give me something, then I am not believing but dreaming because I believe in something that is not factual but my own imagination. From this example, we can see the important relationship between faith and promise.

God's promises are only recorded in God's Word, the Bible. To know the promises of God, one must know the Word of God. Without the promises of God, our faith is not real faith. The promises are in the Word of God. "So faith comes...through the word of Christ" (Rom. 10:17). We have said that we need to believe in God's faithfulness, trustworthiness, and reliability. We have also said that if we know God, we will spontaneously have faith. This is related to God's promises, that is, to His words. If God has not promised anything, how can we know that He is faithful? He must promise something before we can talk about His faithfulness.

What is faith? Faith is holding on to what God has said and praying for God's work to be realized. Faith is believing that God will do what He has said. Faith is believing that God is faithful and that He will work out what He has said. Whether our faith is great or small is not the issue. The issue is: if God has promised something, will He lie and change? The only question we should ask is whether or not we believe that God is honest. This has nothing to do with our faith being great or small.

We know that God loves us. Therefore, we should have no doubt that He is for us. The Bible shows us at least two aspects concerning His promises: "What He [has] promised He [is] able also to do" (Rom. 4:21). God is powerful, and His power fulfills His promises. Our God is not a weak and powerless God who cannot do what He says He will do. If this were so, what good would His promises be? All of His promises would be empty words. But God is not only powerful in promising something, He is also powerful in carrying out His promise. Whatever He has promised, He is able to carry it out. "He is able"—this is what the Bible tells us about His person. "For the Lord is *able* to make him stand" (Rom. 14:4). "God is *able* to make all grace abound unto you" (2 Cor. 9:8). "He is *able* to guard..." (2 Tim. 1:12). Abraham offered up

Isaac because he knew that "God was *able* to raise men even from the dead..." (Heb. 11:19).

God is not only able to do what He has promised to do; He is also intent on doing it. Even if someone has the ability to carry them out but does not keep his words, the promises are vain. God is not only able; He is intent on carrying out His promises. "For He who has promised is faithful" (Heb. 10:23). "If we are faithless, He remains faithful, for He cannot deny Himself" (2 Tim. 2:13). God intends that all of His promises, every word and every sentence, be fulfilled in His children. Whatever He says, He will keep. Whatever He has promised, He will fulfill. Otherwise, His deity would be threatened. Since He cannot deny Himself, He must remain trustworthy whatever the circumstances. If His promises are vain words, we cannot entrust all things and ourselves to God. How can we still doubt if He has promised something, since He is faithful and will not break His words?

Therefore, brothers, please learn this lesson today. You are not the basis of faith. Never ask yourselves, "Do I have faith? Is my faith sufficient?" It is useless to ask such questions. The more you ask, the less faith you will have. Please ask God. What is God's promise concerning this matter? Has His love towards you changed? Will He break His word of promise? Is He able to carry out His promises? Is He trustworthy? Is He reliable? When you consider more about God, you will not have to manufacture faith. Faith will come spontaneously. Remember, you are not trustworthy, and your faith is also not trustworthy. Only God is trustworthy.

CHAPTER SIX

FAITH IN PRACTICE

There are many promises in the Bible. All of these promises are real and can be enjoyed by every saint.

Our God is very powerful and rich. In the stories in the Bible, we see how God worked for His children and stretched forth His mighty arm to save, protect, and guide.

God never changes, and the words of His promises never change. Both God and His promises stand forever. After considering all the work that God has done in the past, we realize that all of His promises in the present are faithful. All the promises in the Bible rest on God's power, love, and faithfulness. If God can change, His promises in the Bible can cease. But if God does not change (thank and praise Him that He never changes), the promises in the Bible will stand forever.

The present error of the saints is that not many of them expect God to do something for them. Many people think that the age of miracles is over. But the Bible is a book for this age. Since it is for this age, the miracles recorded in the Bible are not merely past events. Many young believers, influenced by the unbelieving environment around them, consider that miracles were only possible and only occurred during biblical times; consequently, they no longer expect to see miracles today. The only reason we think this way is because of a lack of faith. We have to realize that all the miracles in the Bible can be repeated today. The most important issue, however, is the believers' faith.

Many people are not inattentive to the question of faith. They talk about faith very much and say with their mouth that they believe. But the most important question is how they believe.

Faith is something that can be put into practice. The reality of faith can only be proved by practice. Faith is not something obscure, but something practical. We should not merely talk about faith with our mouth. We should put our faith into practice. Faith is not merely a spiritual term. It is "the substantiation of things hoped for, the conviction of things not seen" (Heb. 11:1). Faith is a substantiation. It is a conviction. Faith is truly a practical expression of the Christian life.

We speak about faith and say that man ought to have faith in God. But how should one have faith? We have faith in God through the daily things around us. What is faith? Faith is a heart that believes in God through ordinary circumstances. Faith is not abstract; it can be practical.

If we have faith in God, we should not just believe in Him when we encounter extraordinary events and face impossible tasks or absolute perils. This is the way the Gentiles take. It is not the way God's children should take. Not only should we know God as our sovereign Lord, but we should know Him like children know their father. We are constantly under His care and protection. The powers of the heavens are behind us and backing us up so that in all things we can overcome through the divine power.

Faith needs to be put into practice. But where should it be put into practice? Surely it should be practiced in difficult and perilous circumstances. However, even during ordinary times, we should put faith into practice. If God's children cannot commit their bodies to God when they are sick, who will believe that they have faith? If believers cannot trust in God for their material riches, can their faith be found? If believers cannot trust in God's arrangement concerning their occupations, can their professed faith help them? If believers cannot trust in God for problems arising in their families, what use is their faith to them? If believers cannot trust in God in their work to save the sinners, but instead exercise their own strength and other worldly methods, what kind of faith do they have? Faith is something that has to be practiced. Faith can be applied. We can apply all of God's promises to us through faith and make the promises manifest in us.

God promises that He is *Jehovah-Ropheka* (Heb.); He is our Healer (Exo. 15:26). If this is so, why are the believers' medical bills not reduced? Many people say that they are not trusting in their doctors and that they are really trusting in God to heal their sicknesses through medicine. But this is a question of the heart. In our heart, who do we trust? The best test is to ask: if we really have faith, would we be willing to trust solely in God without medicine? If we cannot, I am afraid it is not realistic for us to say that we trust in God in spite of the medicine. If we cannot trust in God without medicine, we cannot trust in Him with medicine. Many times in our sicknesses, we have not thought about God and sought healing apart from God. Even if medicine is not harmful in itself, it is harmful to man in this respect. If we cannot trust in God in our sicknesses, when will we trust in God?

Many people do not dare give up their present position for the Lord's sake. They are afraid that if they give up their position, they will not be able to secure another position. Is the hand of Jehovah so short and the Most High God not able to plan for you? Many faithful children of God have tried God in this matter and realized that He is trustworthy.

Money is another big issue. The biblical teaching is that believers should not be in debt (Rom. 13:8). But how many times have men put themselves under debt at perilous times? If we have faith in God, practical faith, how can we do something that is contrary to scriptural teaching? Why are we unable to wait quietly for God to open up a way for us? If God is the God who feeds the sparrow and cares for the lilies, can He not take care of our food and clothing? If He cared for millions of Israelites in the wilderness and provided warmth and food for them in desperate circumstances, can He not care for us? Are there no more manna and quails today? In reality, God's ravens are flying everywhere. The real problem is that the saints are either in their fat years or their lean years and have not looked to God. Therefore, they do not see God's work. We should either not mention faith at all or put into practice the faith that we mention.

A family encounters numerous problems and difficulties! Yet how many saints trust in God for their family affairs? If, as Job said, "When he giveth quietness, who then can make trouble?" (Job 34:29), why would we not trust in God? How many times has a saint come to God by faith through prayer to commit his family affairs to Him?

If we truly believe in God, why are we so fearful and lost in difficult and dangerous situations? Is not our Lord the Lord of all things? If the universe operates according to His command, will He not have a way to deliver us?

If we examine our daily lives, we will find out how much faith we have! Empty professions of faith will not help us at all. Faith is manifested in the small things in our daily lives.

The Bible is full of promises. For every matter, there are promises in the Bible which guarantee that God will work for us. As long as we have faith, God will work for us.

CHAPTER SEVEN

TALKS ON FAITH

Works without faith are dead. In the same way, faith without works is dead. This is true in the case of the salvation of sinners. It is also true in the case of the believers' living. Our attention today is focused on the Christians' works of faith. The unique place where faith is expressed is in their works. What we do expresses what we believe. If our faith and works do not agree with each other, there must be something wrong with our faith. Many believers do not know how to believe and express their faith. Actually, the matter is quite simple. Faith is expressed through works. "Faith worked together with his works, and by these works faith was perfected" (James 2:22). Suppose a believer merely professes with his mouth. "What is the profit...if anyone says he has faith but does not have works? Can that faith save him?" (v. 14). According to the biblical teaching here, if we believe God in a certain matter, we should have a work of faith in that matter. Otherwise, our faith will not help us receive God's deliverance in that matter.

Two meanings are implied: (1) our work proves our faith, and (2) our work perfects or completes our faith.

If there is faith, there must be works that correspond with the faith. If a man believes that a house is on fire, he will surely not sit still in the house. If he sits still there, he does not believe that the house is on fire. If we commit a matter to the Lord and believe that God will work for us, our attitude toward the matter will surely see a great change. If a man says that he believes that God will work for him, yet busily makes plans himself, being worried and distressed, his faith must be false. "For we who have believed enter into the rest" (Heb. 4:3). Faith and rest cannot be separated from one another. Whenever we truly believe, our heart will be at rest. If our hearts are restless and uneasy, if we are afraid of this and that, and if we are fearful and feeling lost, struggling with all our effort to scheme, plan, resolve, plead, ask for help, and maneuver, then this shows that we have not yet believed. When one believes, he is at rest. Therefore, when a person believes, he will no longer worry or busily plan. Instead, he will be like a weaned child resting in his mother's bosom. There must be works to our faith, and the first step of our work of faith is to stop our own works and rest in God's love, wisdom, and power.

This kind of rest is very real, genuine, and natural. It is not a pretentious calm, unnatural self-restraint, or acting as if nothing has happened. Faith brings in restfulness because of the knowledge that God is for us. "If God is for us, who can be against us?" (Rom. 8:31). Therefore, there is the rest. In addition, we know our own emptiness and that nothing can be accomplished through our designs and laborious schemes. Faith does not rest in itself. God is the place where faith rests. Only those who have such rest have faith. Those who do not have such rest do not have faith. Anything that comes by force is not faith. Faith is something that comes spontaneously. When we see a person, we know he is there. Do we have to contrive to think he is there? Do we have to force ourselves to believe he is there? Do we have to reason and research before we can acknowledge the reality of this fact? Within a second we believe spontaneously. There is no need for us to struggle to believe. This is the way with all kinds of faith. The origin of faith comes from God; it causes our spiritual eyes to discern the reality of a matter. As a result we believe. When we see and know certain things, spontaneously we believe in them. Faith results in rest, and rest comes not from prediction but from foreknowledge. We exercise faith in restfulness, and we rest in faith. Faith is something very spontaneous. Anything that is not spontaneous is not faith.

Of course, there are counterfeits for everything. There is the possibility of a counterfeit for every spiritual experience of the believers. If believers are not careful, they will be deceived. There is no exception to this in the matter of faith.

Many times Satan will deceive the believers, causing them to have false peace and believe in themselves, which is where the problem really lies. They can be convinced that God is going to do certain works. When God does not work, their doubts multiply and they stumble. The believers must realize that true faith is given by God and is for the accomplishment of *God's* will. *Every time* God gives us faith, He gives *evidence* for the faith. It is not a matter of what we think or how we feel, but a matter of what God has said. Sometimes He speaks to us through the holy Word, reveals His view concerning a certain matter, and gives a promise. Faith comes from such a promise. Sometimes He works in our spirit, reveals His will, and gives us His promises in our spirit. Spontaneously, we receive the faith that He has given. The faith that God gives cannot be separated from His promises. However, this does not refer to all the promises of the Bible. It is a matter of whether or not God has given you a particular promise. Nor does this refer to all the sensations in your spirit. Rather, it refers to the promises in which the revelation in our spirit does not contradict the teaching of the Bible. Only the biblical promises that God speaks to us in our spiritual sensations are real. Only the faith that comes out of these promises is reliable. All true faith depends not on what we think, but on what God has *said*.

We said all of this to show that our works should prove our faith. Now we will consider the meaning of our works completing our faith.

When we believe in God, spontaneously we will not worry and strive. We will *not* do these things; this is the negative works of faith. The negative works of faith are important and necessary, but they are not complete. After one has faith, he still needs the positive works of faith. We have previously mentioned that there are things that we should not do. Now, through the power of God, there are things that we should do. Our positive works must match our faith. Furthermore, these works complete our faith, and we receive the promised blessings of God much sooner. This is not a matter of hastiness in the flesh, but an expression of the strength of the power in the spirit. God would like to give us what we need immediately.

But, if the death of our natural life is not substantial and deep enough, an immediate answer would strengthen our soul-life. Until our own life has lost all possibility of being active again, God has to delay what He has long promised. Positive works are a death-blow to our self-life and an expression of the vigor of spiritual strength. Therefore, they will accelerate the accomplishment of God's promises. What are the positive works of faith? They are to walk and act as if we *have* received God's promises. In other words, we believe that something is already accomplished and behave as if it is already accomplished. Let us consider a few matters.

Suppose you are sick. God may give you a personal promise that you will be healed. On the negative side, you should rest in God's work and not disturb His work by any human means. Rather, you should commit yourself to the hand of the Almighty without worry or concern. On the positive side, there are important steps that you should take. You should walk as if you are a healed person. You do not have to wait until you are really healed before you can consider yourself healed. When God gives you the faith to believe that you are healed, at that moment you are healed. If you are healed, you should act like you are healed. Therefore, when you receive faith, you should ask, "How should I act if I am a healed person who has been restored by God? Should I lie on my bed for a long time, or should I stand up to walk?" You should walk as if you are a healed person. However, this must be done after you have received a promise from God and must be carried out in complete reliance on God. Otherwise, the result will be a failure.

The same is true in regards to trusting in God for our living. Although sometimes we may be in great want, what we look toward is a fountain and not a bucket. We should not worry or be tempted to borrow (Rom. 13:8). In the God-ordained principle of giving, we should still be very generous. If we trust in God when we are in trials, we should not tell others, hint at help from others, or resort to other methods. We should live as if nothing has happened. Other matters such as peace within the family, occupations, livelihoods, sufferings, dangers, and other similar matters should follow the same principle. We have to know that God is not only interested in our spiritual affairs; He is equally concerned with the many matters related to our physical being. This is the characteristic of faith: faith does not wait until something is done before believing, because then there is no need to believe anymore. Faith is exercised before something is accomplished and believes, based on God's promises, that it has already been accomplished. The Lord Jesus' teaching concerning faith is, "Believe that you have received them, and you will have them" (Mark 11:24). Faith is not believing after receiving. Rather, it is believing, before ever receiving, that one has received. This is the most profound aspect of the law of faith. Nevertheless, we have mentioned that faith must be expressed through works. Therefore, when one believes that he has received, he should act as if he has received.

Such work is very spontaneous. The eyes of faith do not see dark clouds in the sky. Rather, they see an unchanging sun above the dark clouds. Physical eyes can only see the present darkness, but the eyes of faith can see the light. They do not imagine; they actually see. Is not the light they see more real than the darkness the world sees? Faith despises all dangers, sufferings, and trials, for it knows what the end will be. The work of faith is not a risk but a sure and practical act. It sees what others do not. Although others may consider such acts dangerous, these "dangers" have been well thought through, prayed about, promised by God, and taught by the Scriptures. If a person has not received the teaching of the Scriptures or the promise of the Holy Spirit in his spirit, forcing himself to do such acts is indeed a risk. But for a believer who has truly received God's revelation and has faith, these acts are spontaneous and unpretentious because they are the most natural result of his faith. Although many believers have never heard these teachings yet, God has been leading them this way already. If the work of our faith is something conscious, artificial, and pretentious, we have not yet learned the lesson of faith. Although all the works of faith are beyond human reason, they are carried out according to the principle of one's living. This one has received God's promise and knows what is going to happen. Therefore, he acts ahead of others. The works of faith are often the works that glorify God.

CHAPTER EIGHT

FAITH

In the Bible God demands faith of His children. Without faith we cannot please Him. All spiritual blessings and arrangements in our circumstances can only be received through faith. We marvel that God considers the faith of the believers so important. Without exception, all the aspects of God's full salvation in the Bible are gained by faith. One thing we know: God hates man's own works, whether they are those of a sinner or those of a saint. Anything from ourselves, anything done independently of God, and anything done according to one's own intention by one's own strength, is hateful to God. Many of these things may seem very good in man's eyes, yet God hates them all. The Lord Jesus told us that there is only one who is good—God. In the Lord's eyes, no one is good. Therefore, anything not according to the will of the good God or anything not done through the power of the good God is not good; it is sin. Nothing but God is good. For this reason, every work outside the will and power of God is not good. Hence, all that a believer does must be of God and through God.

Here the matter of faith comes in. Faith has two basic principles: (1) stopping man's own work and (2) waiting for God's work. We commonly think that faith is believing, depending, and waiting for God's work. But there is a step before this, that is, stopping man's work. This stopping of one's own work is the work of faith. Waiting for God to work is something that happens inside a believer and is not visible. But stopping one's own work is something that is outwardly visible at times. The greatest accomplishment of faith is not that God works for the believer, but that the believer stops his own work.

The importance of this step cannot be overemphasized. God has never allowed His own work to be mingled with the work of man's flesh. He demands the believers to totally stop everything that is of the self, whether it be in intention or in ability. He likes to be trusted and entrusted by the believers. How is such a heart of trust in God expressed? It is expressed in an absolute stillness and quietness of the self. This is the first step of the work of faith. Does a man still tire himself with planning and working, after he has fully entrusted a work to his friend? If God is reliable and His power sufficient, does He still need our help? If we believe that God works for us, why are we still anxious? Is it because we are afraid that He will not do well? If so, we have not yet believed. Faith demands that we fully rest. This is a rest in which the heart is free from anxiety and the body free from labor. If there is still restlessness in our heart and body, whether it be anxiety or labor, it shows that we have no faith. The first principle of faith is to stop our own work. If we are still worried from looking at our poor self and our difficult environment, it means that we have never yet relied on God. If we still use our own ability, power, friends, connections, and tact to labor, it means we have not yet realized our uselessness; we have not yet completely committed matters into the hand of God. A life of faith is a life of giving up the self. Acts of faith are but acts of self-surrender. Faith requires us to give up our pettiness with its worries. It also requires us to give up our ability with its accompanying labor. Putting an absolute stop to our own work is the first expression of the work of faith.

It is interesting that this kind of faith does not come from the believer himself. Inasmuch as the faith at our initial salvation was given by God (Eph. 2:8), the faith in our daily life is also given by God. Nothing else is needed to prove how useless a believer can be in himself; we only need to look at the matter of faith in God. The believer himself does not even have faith; he has to receive it from God. All faith is given by God. This is what the apostle meant when he said that faith is one item of the gift of the Holy Spirit.

Are we not many times very willing to believe in God and

fully trust Him in our circumstances? We have heard other brothers telling us that we should exercise faith to believe in God. But no matter how hard we exercise, is it not true that we simply cannot believe? Many times we exert such an effort that it seems as if our hearts are almost bursting. Yet is it not true that this kind of faith produces no effect? We center our whole being on struggling with doubt, yet we still do not reach our goal. Such a situation is most painful. The most difficult time a believer has is when he is struggling with doubt.

This, however, is not faith. Faith cannot be invoked or generated by man, nor can it be brought forth from his heart. Faith is given by God. This faith controls the believer; the believer does not control this faith. Many times, we desire faith in order to achieve something, only to find that there is no way to obtain such faith. At other times, we ourselves have no intention of doing anything, yet God grants us faith and causes this faith to be expressed through our prayer, thus bringing forth the greatest achievement. God does not grant faith to satisfy our cravings. Our rightful position is death, as those who prostrate themselves in the dust. According to the will of God, the saints on the earth should live for His will and glory. It is wrong for a believer to decide, desire, or do anything out of himself. God wants us to be His vessel, but that requires us to die. Even in the matter of believing in God for the fulfillment of a certain work, God wants us to simply be a vessel. When He wants to accomplish something, He grants us the faith to petition in prayer for His work. Only then will He move to accomplish the work. Of course, this is a suffering to the flesh, because there is no possibility for its activity and no room for its craving. But since a true believer lives only for God and not for himself, he is happy and willing to simply be a dead instrument to accomplish the supreme will of God.

See what wisdom God has! If faith were ours, something that came from within us, it would be possible for us to direct our faith. In other words, if *we* wanted something carried out, all we would have to do is believe a little, and we would get God's work done. But this is not the way faith works.

Faith is given by God. Before God gives faith, there is no way for us to believe. Many of us have experienced that we often had no way to enter into rest because we could not produce faith. Then suddenly God would grant us faith. (Sometimes this comes through one or two verses; sometimes it comes after prayer, when a believer understands the will of God in his intuition.) When this happens, we are immediately assured, and our hearts are spontaneously calmed down. It *seems* that we have the assurance that God will definitely accomplish His work. There is no need for struggling. There is no need for anxiety. There is not even the need to worry about exercising. Assurance simply comes spontaneously without invitation. When God grants faith this way, the believer immediately has the work of faith, that is, rest without anxiety. Any other way is not faith and will never give rest.

At this point, we must clarify something. To say what we have said does not mean that we can now neglect everything and simply wait for the visitation of this faith. There are two kinds of faith: special faith and general faith. Special faith is a kind of faith granted by God for a special matter. It is a faith which believes that God *will surely accomplish* a certain matter for us. We do not have this kind of faith in every situation. General faith is the *daily* faith of an experienced believer toward God. This kind of faith is not directed towards any special matter, but it is directed towards *all things.* Such a believer believes that whatever God does *can never be wrong.* He believes that whether it be failure or success, God's good pleasure is there. Although we do not always have special faith in everything that happens to us, we should have general faith. We must believe that our God does everything right and that everything is in His hand. He knows whether it is good for us to suffer or succeed. We should have this kind of general faith all the time. Even when special situations arise, we should not lose this kind of faith. But regardless of which kind of faith we have, faith should always have its manifestation in our conduct; there should always be rest for those who have faith; and there should also be no struggle and fleshly energy in trying to help God.

CHAPTER NINE

ADDITIONAL WORD TO THE ARTICLE "THE FAITH OF ABRAHAM"

Abraham is our model. God wants to lead and guide us, as He did Abraham, into Canaan, a place full of idols and often in famine. In this place only a small parcel of land belongs to us. Here Satan is the ruler of everything, and little fruit is produced from the land. Everything in such an environment seems to speak contrary to God's promise, and it seems unlikely that God would have brought us to such a place. Is this what we get for leaving behind our old way of life, kindred, and country? Where is the land and the seed that God has promised? What did Abraham see in that day? He saw nothing. Year after year until he died, he only begot Isaac. Of the numerous descendants promised to him, who would be as many as the stars in heaven, the sands by the sea, and the dust on the earth, he only saw Isaac! When his wife died, he did not have one plot of land in which to bury her. He had to buy a burial ground. Is this what God had promised? Yet the father of our faith did not doubt. He knew what faith was and what it was to not live by sight. He followed God. Abraham can see now and will see the complete fulfillment of God's promises in the kingdom to come. Today is there anything that man can see and feel elated about? This is the way God leads every one of His faithful believers to take. Although we see and feel nothing today, the future will be full of spiritual land and descendants.

[Editor's note: An article, "The Faith of Abraham," was written by Ruth Lee and included in the same issue of the magazine.]

CHAPTER TEN

FAITH AND OBEDIENCE

Scripture Reading: Rom. 6:11-14

Today I will speak about the principles of Christian living. The entire New Testament shows us that there are only two principles of Christian living; everything else is merely fruit that issues from these two principles. Patience, meekness, truthfulness, temperance, and whatever else are not the principles of Christian living. There are only two principles of Christian living: one is faith; the other is obedience. All good fruit issues from these two principles. In our fellowship with the Lord, we need faith and obedience every day.

In the New Testament, many verses speak about faith and obedience. I will only mention Romans 6:11 and 13. Verse 11 says "reckon." This is faith. Verse 13 says "present." This is obedience. Verse 11 speaks of faith in reference to what Christ has accomplished. Verse 13 speaks of presenting our members to God, which will preserve the ground we gain through faith. If we can balance the principles of faith and obedience, all spiritual experiences will open before us, and we will be able to enter into these experiences freely.

What are faith and obedience? All the objective truths are in Christ and have been accomplished. All the subjective truths are in the Holy Spirit and will be accomplished by Him. I do not know if all of you understand the difference between redemption and salvation. Redemption was accomplished more than nineteen hundred years ago, while salvation was accomplished on the day you believed in the Lord. Therefore, redemption is objective; it has been accomplished in Christ. Salvation is subjective; it is what the Holy Spirit accomplishes in us. The order of these two matters cannot be reversed. The Lord Jesus did not accomplish salvation nineteen hundred years ago, neither did the Spirit within me accomplish redemption today. One was accomplished long ago; the other is waiting to be accomplished. Suppose I have not yet believed in the Lord. When you preach the gospel to me, you can only say that redemption has been accomplished; you cannot say that salvation has been accomplished, because I have not yet been saved. Salvation is accomplished only after I have believed in the Lord, but redemption was accomplished long before I believed in the Lord. All the redemptive work is past. All the objective works are in the past; they are absolute and eternal. All subjective works are accomplished in the present and in the future. One has been accomplished; the other is waiting to be accomplished. On the one hand, death, burial, resurrection, and ascension are accomplished. On the other hand, the death which the Holy Spirit puts within you is accomplished only when you believe. The resurrection of Christ took place more than nineteen hundred years ago, but it is manifested in you on the day you believe. Everything objective is in the past; it is absolute, complete, and nothing can be added. Everything subjective is accomplished in the present and in the future. Receiving something objective and receiving something subjective require two completely different principles. Since the objective has been accomplished, we should just believe. Since the subjective is accomplished now and in the future, we need to obey. If we pay attention only to one side, we will go astray by either becoming theoretical or ascetic. The objective death, resurrection, and ascension require our believing. However, it is not enough just to believe. Day by day we also need to obey. Crucifixion with Christ requires obedience; the power of resurrection requires obedience; and the place of ascension requires obedience.

Brothers and sisters, we need an outward Savior and an inward Savior. We need the Word incarnated in the flesh and the Word manifested in the Holy Spirit. We need the Christ of Golgotha and the Christ in the Spirit. The Savior who is without demands our faith, whereas the Holy Spirit who is within demands our obedience. Now I would like to speak about some experiences in order for us to understand faith and obedience.

What does believing mean? This is something that we cannot give up even for a single day. Objective truths need our believing. A man should not say that he needs to die, resurrect, and ascend. Rather, he should say that he has died, resurrected, and ascended. What is faith? Faith means that you have known, seen, and acknowledged. A man cannot believe in what he has not seen. Whether it is death, resurrection, or ascension, there must first be the revelation of the Holy Spirit before there can be the faith. A doctrine is a presentation of the facts, while a truth is the reality behind what is presented. Many times, many doctrines are not truths to us. When something is really there, it will not only be a doctrine, but a truth. The death of the Lord Jesus on our behalf is not only a doctrine, but also a truth. Theology is about doctrines. In other words, doctrines are theology. The objective truth requires that we believe. We must know that it is real. In Greek, *truth* means reality. The death of the Lord is a truth, which means that the death of the Lord is a reality. The resurrection of the Lord is a truth, which means that the resurrection of the Lord is a reality. The ascension of the Lord is a truth, which means that the ascension of the Lord is a reality. This is what we call the truth.

How do we know that these truths are real? Every time we receive a truth, it is not due to what was said by the preacher. The only One in the whole world who can bring men into the truth is the Holy Spirit. Preachers can only speak doctrines to men, but there must be the revelation of the Holy Spirit before men can have faith. Brothers and sisters, have we seen this? I am not speaking about our death, resurrection, and ascension with Christ. I am only speaking about the Lord's death on our behalf. In the past we did not know sin, neither did we know God or Christ. Perhaps one day when we heard someone speak about the death of the Lord Jesus on our behalf, there was one word that touched our heart. As a result we said, "Oh, that is what this is!" Suddenly we "saw" sin, we "saw" God, we "saw" Christ, and we "saw" salvation. We saw that our sins were forgiven, and

we had the boldness to say that our sins were forgiven. Someone might have asked us how we knew our sins were forgiven.
Despite their question, we were very clear about it because
we had seen.

What is the revelation of the Holy Spirit? It is the Holy
Spirit removing the veil and showing you what lies behind a
preacher's speaking. You may have seen what is meant by forgiveness and regeneration. This seeing is most precious.
When you saw that Christ Jesus died in such a way, you
believed. You may go to the countryside and see an old friend
and preach to him. He may nod his head, but soon forget what
you preached. He lacks one necessary thing; he has not
obtained the revelation. Those who are blind cannot believe.
Those who have no revelation cannot have faith. You must
pray that God will make him see his sin and see the Savior.
You may have preached three or five doctrines to him. But
when he sees, there is no need to preach to him anymore. Just
as he needs to see Christ's death, he also needs to see resurrection, ascension, and all the other truths.

Brothers, you may go to the countryside to preach the
gospel to fifty people and tell them how man sinned, how
the Lord died for man, and how faith brings in salvation. All
fifty people may nod their heads. However, does this mean
that all fifty are saved? Although they nod their heads, they
walk away with no realization that lying and pride are sins.
They have heard about sin but have not seen sin. They
have heard about the Savior but have not seen the Savior.
Thus, there is no possibility for them to believe. Every time
we preach the gospel to someone, we must ask God to open
their eyes so that they will weep at seeing their sin and
receive the Lord when they see Him. After some time a theo-
logical professor may come and tell them that their sins are
not really sins and that the Lord's death was merely an act of
self-sacrifice. However, they will not be moved if they have
seen something. They believe because they have seen something.

Death is an objective truth. It demands our believing. All
the other objective truths also demand our believing. We have
paid considerable attention to preaching the Lord's death.

Nevertheless, it has not been effective. Something is wrong in the matter of faith, and this means something is wrong with the revelation. Once I preached about the truth of our crucifixion with the Lord. A brother said that it was good and that he would be victorious from then on because he now knew the way to victory. I said that after a few days it would not work because he had not yet seen. You may ask someone how they were saved, and they may say that they heard the teaching. However, this kind of salvation will not last for more than a few days. Mere understanding in the mind is not faith. When you read the Bible or hear in the meeting that you have died, resurrected, and ascended, you should not say, "I have examined myself and have not found any resurrection or ascension." Neither should you say lightly, "I have died, resurrected, and ascended." Instead, you should ask the Lord, "Make me see that I have died, resurrected, and ascended." If you pray in this way, the Lord will usher you into the objective truth, that is, into Himself. You will see that *in Christ,* you are dead, resurrected, and ascended. Since He has died, you also have died; since He has resurrected, you also have resurrected; and since He has ascended, you also have ascended. In this way you will say, "Lord, I thank You. In You I have died, resurrected, and ascended." You will say this because of faith. This faith is based on the facts behind the words.

Mr. Hudson Taylor was at one time continuously experiencing failure and weakness. Once he wrote to his sister about how his heart was very troubled because he felt that he was lacking sanctification, life, and power within. He thought that if he could only abide in Christ, everything would be fine. His sister prayed for him. For a few months he prayed, struggled, fasted, made resolutions, read the Bible, and used more time for quiet meditation. However, nothing was effective. He wished he could abide in Christ forever, but it seemed that after dwelling in Him for a short while, he came out again. He said, "If I only knew I could abide in Christ, then everything would be well; but I could not." From his diary we read the following story: one day he was praying again. He thought that if he could abide in Christ and could draw His juice and receive His nourishment and supply, he would have the power to overcome sin. He prayed again and read the Bible again. Then he came to John 15:5, which says, "I am the vine; you are the branches." He said, "I am the most foolish man in the whole world. I have been praying to be a branch; I wanted to abide in Christ. However, the Lord has said that I *already* am a branch and abiding in Him." O brothers, if we realize this, we will say, "Hallelujah!" We do not need to enter anything, because we are already in. We do not need to strive to be a branch, nor do we become a branch only after we have overcome sin. We are already a branch, and we are abiding in Him. The purpose of John 15:5 is to tell us that we are abiding in Him and that we should not leave this abiding. We are a branch. All the juice, nourishment, and love are ours. Mr. Taylor said that since he saw this, he became a new Hudson Taylor. This was a great turning point in his life.

Believing is not changing God's word into reality. It is believing that God's word is reality. During last year's special conference, I mentioned that the grace of God comprises three things: the promise, the fact, and the covenant. The promise is something which will be accomplished. The fact is something which has been accomplished. All the objective truths have been accomplished and are real. We only need to say to God, "Your Word says I have died, resurrected, and ascended. Therefore, I also say that I have died, resurrected, and ascended." Indeed, this is the way we can stand firm. God has spoken, and it is so.

Mr. _____ was a famous speaker in the Keswick Conventions. The turning point of his life was due to one incident. Once he chose 2 Corinthians 12:9, "My grace is sufficient for you," to be the topic of his message. After he had prepared the outline, he knelt down to pray, "I respectfully present the draft of this message before You. O God! I pray for Your blessings." After the prayer he realized that he could not use this message. "I was going to preach to the people that the grace of God is sufficient for us. But if anyone would ask me whether the grace of God is sufficient for me, I would definitely have to say no because I still have my temper and pride. If the grace of God is not sufficient for me, how can I say to people that it is sufficient for them? I cannot say that."

It was Saturday, there was no time to prepare for anything else, and he did not have the choice not to preach. Confronted with this difficult situation, he knelt down and prayed again, "O God! Today let Your grace be sufficient for me. May this become my own experience. I have been proud, jealous, lustful, and filled with unclean thoughts. Make me overcome all these if Your grace is truly sufficient for me." He prayed the whole afternoon, but it seemed the more he prayed, the further God was away from him. Later he became tired and walked from his desk to the side of the fireplace for a rest. There on the wall by the fireplace hung a verse saying, "My grace IS sufficient for you." Immediately he became clear that the grace of God is not "going to be sufficient for me," nor "awaiting to be sufficient for me," but rather it "is sufficient for me." He did not need to ask God to give him sufficient grace; God's grace *was* sufficient for him. He jumped to his feet and said, "The grace of God *is* sufficient for me. Why do I have to pray?" This is faith, and this is also a revelation. He said, "Thank God, for many years I always anticipated sufficient grace from God. On that day God revealed to me that His grace *is* sufficient. I came to a great turning point in my life." The next day he was exceptionally powerful. Later in the Keswick Convention, he gave many messages and helped many people. Someone asked him how he became the way he was. He answered that he had seen the *sufficiency.*

There are many people who pray for death with Christ, but God says that in Christ we are dead. There are many who pray for resurrection and ascension, but God says that in Christ we are resurrected and ascended. There are many who pray to overcome the world, but the Word of God says that the victory which has overcome the world is our faith (1 John 5:4). Everything is in Christ. We must see this in order to believe. Suppose there is a brother or a sister here who has seen the objective truth. They may not have seen many things, but as long as they see one verse and truly believe in it, they can walk in the path before them. Many people make blind requests to God. Have you heard of sinners asking the Lord to die for them? Once when I was preaching the gospel, I heard someone pray in this way: "O Lord! I am a sinner. I ask that You die on my behalf." This prayer is wrong. There are many people who pray for the Lord to die for them or that they would die together with the Lord. This is utterly a joke. The mind is really useless. We must believe in God's Word more than our circumstances, feelings, trials, sins, lusts, and unclean thoughts. If we can do this, we definitely will be different. It is not enough that we listen. We must have the faith. May we see that God has accomplished everything in Christ.

However, we have to know that merely believing like this is not enough. The one thing that has to follow is obedience. On the one hand, we must believe. On the other hand, we must obey. Our self-will must be subdued, and we must present every member to God. Brothers and sisters, after we have a living faith, day by day we have to learn to obey God. Whenever God touches us on a certain point, and instead we want God to go along with us, we are not obeying God. Whenever our will is not subdued, we are unable to believe God. A sinner who does not repent cannot believe. Likewise, a believer who willfully does not obey cannot believe.

Some have many things stored in their houses. Some are hesitant to consecrate their children. Some do not have a right attitude towards their husbands. Some do not exercise proper stewardship of their money. Have you consecrated yourself to God? Are you willing to go wherever God sends you? If God wants you to do the most trivial job, are you willing to do it? Brothers and sisters, believing alone cannot keep you walking on the path ahead. Perhaps God wants you to obey immediately after you have believed, or He may wait a little while before He asks you to obey. With some people the Lord wants them to obey Him first, and then He gives them the faith. With other people God first gives them the faith, and then He demands obedience. With still others God gives them faith and at the same time demands their obedience.

I do not know what the Lord requires from each one of us. But I know that there is a great lack if we only have one of these two aspects. Anyone who has not presented his body to God and thinks that believing alone is sufficient is like an unturned cake. May we see that we must obey God. We must pass this step in a specific way. This is a hurdle. In order to be God's stewards, we must have a specific starting point. There must be a point at which we say to God, "From today on, I offer myself to You." There must be a specific dealing this way. There must be a time when we say to God, "From now on I offer You my time, my mind, my money, my family, and my all." God touches everyone in a specific way. With some, God touches them on one point; with others, God touches them on another point. Many times God's demand appears to be harsh and severe. But whatever God demands of us, we must obey. God wants us to prove that we will obey Him. Nothing is more precious to Him than Isaac. It is not enough just to say verbally, "I offer Isaac as a sacrifice." We must present Isaac as an offering in reality. If we do this, we will see the lamb God has prepared. God is not satisfied until we have fully obeyed. We must experience specific dealings with the Lord.

We have an American friend who was once in China. His faith is truly great. The way the Lord led him to advance spiritually was as follows: He had a master's degree, but he continued working in the university toward a doctorate of philosophy. He was a pastor and studying philosophy at the same time. He felt something wrong with his spiritual life, and he prayed to God, "I have a great deal of unbelief on many occasions. I cannot overcome some sins, and I do not have the power in the work." For two weeks he specifically prayed for God to fill him with the Holy Spirit. He wanted to acquire the victorious life and power spoken of in the Bible. God told him then, "Do you really want this? If you really do, two months from now you should not take the examination for the doctorate of philosophy. I have no use for a doctorate of philosophy." He felt that this was rather difficult. His doctorate of philosophy was something he definitely wanted. It would indeed be a pity if he did not go for the examination. He knelt down to pray and bargain with the Lord. He asked why He would not let him be a doctor of philosophy and a pastor as well. But God never bargains with man. Once God has made a demand, that is the demand. What God has said and commanded cannot be changed. During those two months, he was in considerable turmoil. When the last Saturday came, he was in a real battle. Should he choose the doctorate of philosophy, or should he choose the filling of the Holy Spirit? Is it better to have a doctorate of philosophy, or have a victorious life? If others can earn a doctorate of philosophy and at the same time be used by God, why could he not do the same? He continuously struggled and bargained with the Lord to no avail. A doctorate of philosophy was desirable; the filling of the Holy Spirit was also desirable. However, God would not yield. If he wanted a doctorate of philosophy, he could not live a spiritual life. If he wanted a spiritual life, he could not have his doctorate of philosophy. In the end, he said in tears, "I obey. Although I have studied philosophy for over two years, and for the past thirty some years since my childhood, I have looked forward to a doctorate in philosophy, I have to give up this pursuit for the sake of obeying God." He wrote a letter to notify the school that he was not going to take the examination on Monday. Thus, he forsook his doctorate of philosophy degree forever. The next day he did not have a message on the pulpit because he was very tired from the previous night. So he simply related to the congregation the story of his obedience to the Lord. On that day, three-fourths of the people in the congregation shed tears and were revived. He himself was also very empowered. He said that had he foreseen this result, he would have obeyed God's leading much sooner.

No one used by the Lord can ever avoid this kind of crisis. If we wish to avoid this kind of crisis, we cannot expect to experience progress in the spiritual life. We must believe and also obey. Not only do we need to obey once, but we must obey continuously. Otherwise, we will come short and be unbalanced. Obedience without faith is powerless. Faith without obedience is idealistic. It is very painful to be obedient without faith. Please remember the scriptural principles for our living: believing and obeying. We cannot believe without obeying or obey without believing. To believe and yet not obey is false belief. To obey and yet not believe is asceticism. Today in the Lord's church, men either err in faith or in obedience.

Every failure is the result of a shortage in one of the two or in both. There is either faith without obedience or obedience without faith, or there is neither faith nor obedience.

If we are willing to believe and obey, we will experience a long-lasting spring and an eternal sunshine. The path of the righteous is like the dawning light growing brighter and brighter until the high noon. May God bless us and make us perfect men before Him, that is, may we be men who will believe and obey.

CHAPTER ELEVEN

LIVING BY FAITH

Scripture Reading: Heb. 10:38

The word "live" in this verse can be translated two ways according to the Greek. It can be translated "have life," or "live." In Romans 1 it should be translated "have life," while in Hebrews it should be translated "live." Because Romans talks about sinners, "live" should be translated "shall have life by faith." Hebrews is written to the believers, those who are saved and have eternal life; therefore, the more accurate translation is "live by faith."

I have met many believers who have mentioned various spiritual problems. Of all of the spiritual problems, there is one that many people have difficultly overcoming. Many believers frequently wonder why at times they feel spiritually dry and tasteless, while at other times they are happy and excited. When they are happy and excited, even though they are not having the experience in the third heaven, it seems as if they are having a unique mountaintop experience. They wonder how they can overcome the dry life to remain all the time in a happy and excited condition. They wish that their whole life would be one of constant flowing and bubbling. If they could do this, they would be able to sing hallelujahs all their life. Many believers are seeking a solution to this problem.

Believers ordinarily refer to this type of living as "wave-like." They live a fluctuating life. In their feelings, many Christians live a life that is sometimes on the mountaintop and sometimes in the valley. Sometimes they are on the top of the wave, and sometimes they are under the waterline. Sometimes they are high, and sometimes they are low. Almost every Christian feels that he is living a fluctuating life. Sometimes he feels very happy and will not be satisfied with only two hours of prayer. The more he testifies, the more he has to say, and the words come out like a river. When he listens to a message, he feels very interested and does not become tired at all. When he studies the Bible, he feels that God's Word is as sweet as honey. But then sometimes, things seem to be completely different. He feels that praying is the same as not praying. Whether or not he prays does not seem to make much difference. The Bible seems to be letters of black and white only, and it is dry and tasteless. When he meets someone, he feels guilty if he does not testify, and so he reluctantly says a few words like, "If you believe in Jesus, you will have eternal life." However, in his heart he feels uninspired and has nothing to say. Other things of the same nature are done halfheartedly. Sometimes he feels that it is only profitable to draw near to God and pray to Him and that no work is necessary. Yet at other times he feels that even this is too dry, and there is not much joy in drawing near to God. Since he feels obligated to draw near to God, however, he does it reluctantly.

We can compare this kind of Christian life to nature. Where there is a mountain, there must be a valley. Where there is a high wave, there is also a low wave. Because many Christians frequently have this kind of experience, they conclude that a fluctuating life is inevitable and that it is impossible to live a steady life. They think that this will be their experience until they die. There is another group of Christians who say that mountain and valley, high and low wave experiences are unnecessary and that the Christian experience of life can be steady and on a straight line. What I want to tell you is that it is not altogether right to say that a Christian must have fluctuating and wavy experiences, nor is it altogether right to say that a Christian's experience must always be level and flat.

If we want to find out the principle of something, we have to combine the experiences of all kinds of people. Only by combining the spiritual experiences of all kinds of people can we come up with a common principle. For example, a person may study patients who have suffered from a certain illness. He will study the causes, symptoms, and results of many cases before he can draw a conclusion. If the hundreds or thousands of patients that are studied are found to have the same cause and same result, he can then draw a conclusion from what is common in all the cases. For this reason, we have to study how the highs and lows of a Christian life occur and how they develop before we can find out the proper principle.

A Christian begins his life from the time he is saved. Is a person sad when he is saved? No, he is very happy. When someone finds a treasure, he is happy. When someone tells you that believing in Jesus Christ will give you eternal life and that you will pass from death to life and never come under condemnation anymore, that is the happiest day of your life. But let me ask, can this happiness remain forever? No, after a while this happy feeling will go away. How long will the happiness last? It is not certain, and it differs from person to person. According to my knowledge, the happy feeling and great joy that one had at the time of salvation seldom lasts more than a few months. Generally speaking, after a month or two, the feeling goes away. With some, the feeling of joy from salvation is gone in only a matter of one or two weeks.

Let us use a horizontal line to illustrate the experiences of a Christian. Anything above this line is joy, and anything below this line is dryness. When some are saved, for the first few months they live in joy. But one morning, though they study the Bible, pray, and fellowship just as before, they feel that their joy is not as full as the day before. It has diminished. Some people are persecuted and ill-treated after they are saved. Others want to deal with their sins to the extent that they are willing to cut off their right arm after they are saved. Still others want to confess their sins to others and give up their sins after they are saved. At this time they are happy and consider it worthwhile to be saved because their happiness more than compensates for their loss. Of course, they should be happy when they are saved. Even God is happy that they are saved. But a few months later, they begin to lose their joy, or the joy is no longer as full as it was before. At the time of salvation, they loved to read the Bible. Even though they may not understand the meaning of the Bible, they are interested in reading it. Although there are many things that new believers do not understand about the Bible, they like to eat and do not think that it is too much to read more than a dozen chapters a day. At that time they feel very happy about praying. Although they cannot tell how many times God has answered their prayer, they still like to pray. They lock themselves up in a room for a few hours and jump up and down for joy. But when the joy is gone, they begin to feel sad. Temptation will come from two sides. On the one side, the enemy will come; Satan will tell them that they are backslidden and no longer saved. On the other side, they will think that they have committed some sins and have become fallen. Yet in spite of their searching, they cannot find out what sins they have committed. Now, they feel that everything has dried up.

However, this dryness does not last long. Sometimes it lasts for one or two weeks; sometimes it goes away in three to five days. Once the dryness goes away, the joy comes back. Formerly, their reading of the Bible and praying were such an effort and drag that it felt like trying to recite a forgotten passage. Now it seems that the fellowship with God is resumed. But how the recovery came about, they do not know. Now they are more careful to maintain their joy. They try their best to maintain the exciting joy. They are more careful in reading the Bible, praying, and testifying to others.

But not long after this, the joy is gone again. They wonder why today is not the same as the day before, for they read the Bible, pray, and testify just the same. Why is there such a big difference between the two days? Why was there the joy yesterday but not today? Under such a condition, they even wonder what God is like and what Jesus Christ is like. They have fallen into a great error. They think that their spiritual power is gone and that they have become fallen. Although they pray, it is not done faithfully; although they read the Bible, they spend less time on it; and although they testify, they do so only reluctantly.

After a few days or several weeks, however, the joy strangely returns. Now they feel an interest in everything again. If they are not having the experience of the third heaven, they are, at least, having a mountaintop experience. But stranger than this is the fact that after a while, they revert to their former dry and tasteless condition. They begin to conclude that their spiritual life is one of ups and downs. If someone asks them about their spiritual life, they would say that their life is fluctuating. During the highs, they read the Bible, pray, and testify with interest and joy, and during the lows, they do the same things without any interest and in dryness. This is the fluctuating life.

I would like to consider the matter of this fluctuation, starting from the first joy we received at the time of salvation. If we can find the cause of the illness, we can find the cure. From the experience of many saved people, we can find a law that joy is greater at the beginning than at the end, while dryness is greater at the end than at the beginning. The joy becomes less intense (though deeper), and the time of joy becomes shorter. At the same time, the dryness becomes more intense and lasts longer (though shallower). Perhaps the first dryness lasts for three to five days; the second dryness for a week; the third for two weeks, and the fourth for perhaps a month. In other words, the second time around, the joy is less intense and shorter than the first, while the dryness is more intense and longer than the first. The period of dryness extends longer, and its intensity increases more. All believers have this kind of experience. Eventually, our dryness is more than our joy.

Can any Christian say that he has more joy today than on the day he was saved? We may feel sad in our hearts and feel that we have sinned or failed. We are not as joyful as when we were first saved. When we were first saved, it was like riding on a cloud or like standing on a mountaintop. We were bold to testify without fear, even on the street. We could read fifty to sixty chapters of the Bible a day and still feel that this was not sufficient. But today we feel that we are dragging our feet in everything we do, and we are reluctant to do anything.

Let me say that we have made a basic mistake. We have a big misconception concerning spiritual experiences; we think that the joyful times are the peak times of our spiritual life.

But the dry times are not times of spiritual decline. Suppose I lost a watch. When I find the watch again, I will become very happy. After three to five days, my joy will not be as great as when I first found the watch. Perhaps after a few days, the joy will be completely gone. But this does not mean that I have lost my watch again. What has been lost is merely the joy of finding the watch. The same is true with our spiritual life. When we found the Savior, we were saved and could not help but rejoice. Not only did we rejoice from ourselves, God gave us joy as well. If someone did not have joy when he was saved, I doubt that he has found the Savior yet. But later the joy was lost. We may think that the things that we gained are lost. Actually, only the joy is lost; the things we gained are not lost. Let me ask: Has the Lord Jesus changed? No. Has God changed? No. Has the eternal life that God has given us been taken back? No. They were ours when we were excited about them. They are still ours when we feel so dry. It does not matter how excited we are or how dry we are. What we gained has not been lost; it is still there. This is why I say that there are no fluctuations in a Christian's life and experience. (This does not include the case of those Christians who have sinned, fallen, or backslidden. Those are exceptions. What we are talking about are the normal conditions of Christians.)

God never changes, the work of the Lord Jesus never changes, and the Holy Spirit never changes. The eternal life that we have received is still there; it is never lost. What is lost is merely our initial joy. A young child may think that the sun is gone when it rains. He may go to his father and ask, "Where is the sun?" He may go up to the roof and find that the sun is not there. He may go to a nearby watchtower and find that the sun is not there. But the sun has not changed; it has merely been blocked by the dark clouds. Today our Sun has not changed; what has changed is our feelings. The sun in the sky has not changed at all. But there are dark clouds in the sky which block the sunlight. If we live in our feelings, our sky will always change, and there will always be the covering of the clouds. If we do not live in our feelings, there will be no change in our sky. We ought to live above the clouds of our feelings.

I have said that the intensity of joy decreases while the duration is shorter, and the intensity of dryness increases while the duration is longer. These are common phenomena of a Christian's experience; they are not accidental. The experience of most Christians falls under this pattern. We can conclude that these things do not happen by accident. Since they do not happen by accident, there must be a hand behind everything. Whose hand? It must be God's hand. He causes our joy to become less intense and its duration to become shorter. He causes our dryness to become more intense and its duration to become longer. (We are merely referring to the experiences of ordinary Christians; we are not talking about the experiences of abnormal or outstanding Christians.)

Abnormal Christians have sinned and become fallen. Of course they have no joy. Outstanding Christians have denied themselves from the beginning in a specific way and pursued after God in a specific way. Every time they go through some special dealing, they experience special joy. Every time they see God working in a special way, they experience special joy. Outstanding Christians and abnormal Christians are exceptions. What we are talking about are the normal Christians.

GOD'S PURPOSE

God's purpose for doing all these things are:

A. That We Would Not Be for Ourselves

When we read the Bible during a period of excitement and joy, we have a great interest in reading. But are we reading the Bible because of our interest or because the Bible is the Word of God? Is the purpose of our prayer to seek God in His presence, or is the goal the joy we feel in our prayer? Are we praying at the expense of forsaking our duty, or are we praying for God's sake? If we do all these things for ourselves and to satisfy ourselves, then our aim is not God's glory. At the height of our excitement, we do not realize that we are doing these things for ourselves; we think that we are doing these things for God. We have to realize that the times we are most excited, when we seem to be living on the mountaintop, perhaps are the times when we are in our flesh the most! This is why God takes our joy away and puts us in a condition of dryness. How do we feel then? Our prayer, reading of the Word, and witnessing become dry. Under these conditions, God is teaching us a lesson; He makes us realize that our peak spiritual experiences are just something of ourselves. We may think that they are the most spiritual experiences. Little do we realize that they are merely of the flesh. Toward the world, we expressed the part of our flesh that is evil. Now we try to express the part of our flesh that is good. God is testing us to see if we will keep praying, reading the Word, and testifying for Him during the times when the joy is gone and the dryness is present. God does not want the dryness to be too harsh for us, so He gives back the joy after a while. But He also does not want us to presume that we have reached the peak of our spirituality, so He takes the joy away again. God does not want us to be discouraged because of the dryness, so that we will not want to be Christians anymore. Therefore, He gives us a little joy again and recovers our taste to a certain degree.

When the dryness comes the second time, God will see if we have learned anything. We may think that we have done something wrong again. Actually, this is not God's intention. He is seeing if we are working according to our duty, or if we are working because of joy. Perhaps some people have to go through these experiences five or six times; perhaps others seven or eight times. Most of the time, the feelings alternate between joy and dryness. This cycle will continue until God arrives at His purpose of causing us to realize that our desire for joy is for ourselves and not for God. This is the first reason God deals with us with joy and dryness.

B. Disciplining the Power of the Will

When we are living a life full of joy on the mountaintop, do we feel that we must exert any effort? We do not feel this. We do not exert any effort in reading the Word, in praying, and in testifying. Suppose we are talkative. During the times when we are happy, when we feel that God is so near us that we can almost touch the Lord Jesus and God, we would rather lock ourselves in a room and not see anybody. At such times, we can easily overcome our natural weaknesses. Suppose we are quick-tempered and very easily lose our temper. During the times when we are excited, we can very easily forgive others. But when the joy is gone, we are like porcupines; others cannot touch us. If they do, we become angry. When we are excited, we do not feel any burden to our work or living. But when we are dry, we feel that all our living and our work are burdensome. At such times it is an exercise of the will for us to read the Word, pray, or testify. At this time we feel that we have to exert much effort and that it is a duty to read the Bible, pray, and testify. Originally in testifying for the Lord, we could speak for five hours according to our excited feelings. But in our dryness we can find nothing to say. We speak about believing in the Lord and receiving eternal life in a restricted way. We have to take control of ourselves to speak something. When we are doing it at the height of our excitement, no effort is involved. But when we feel dry, we consider such work to be extremely burdensome, and we are not able to do it except with much determination. Let me ask: During which time do we experience actual spiritual dealings? It is when we are dry. When we are excited, we may not have any spiritual experience but only the results from the power of our emotion. When we are dry, we have to exercise our *will,* and our work is the result of our real person. The reason God gives us the dryness is so that we will learn to exercise our will during these dry times.

Suppose we are traveling by a sailboat from one place to another. The journey may take only a few hours. At the beginning of the journey, the wind blows in the right direction, and we hoist the sail. After a while the wind stops, but there are still a few hours to go. Should we take out our oars and row, or should we anchor and wait until a good wind comes before we set sail again? If we want to reach our destination sooner, we have to try our best to row. At such times we are exerting the true strength we have. This is only an illustration. When we are excited in our emotion, we are like a boat sailing with the wind; the boat does not have to exert any effort. We wish that there could be smooth sailing all year round. But if this were the case, both the captain and the sailors of a ship would become useless; they would only be able to sail in favorable winds. If the direction of the wind changed, they would not know what to do. I am afraid no one would want these sailors. When God gives us favorable wind, we praise Him. But He is also stirring us up to exercise the resurrection power given to us, without which we would not move when the joy is gone. God gives us the dryness, so that when joy and excitement are not present, we would exercise our own strength (the strength we received at the time of our regeneration). In this way, we will be able to pass through hindrances and contrary winds. The power of resurrection is more clearly demonstrated in an environment filled with death.

God can grant us the help of emotions, but this is not His purpose. The help of emotions is merely the means by which God deals with us. His intention is to train our will, so that at the darkest hour, we could still exercise our will, and at the time when we feel dry, we could still exercise our will to read the Bible, pray, and testify. By doing this, the strength of our will will become stronger and stronger. If we only move by the power of the emotion, we will never advance. The reason God gives us feelings of joy is so that we would not turn back halfway in our Christian life. This is why the joy we receive from Him diminishes to a shorter time as we go on, and the dryness increases for a longer period of time. We will then exercise our will more, and our will, will be greatly strengthened.

When we examine our past experiences, we see that our joy and dryness fluctuate. We also learn that during the times of joy, there is not much progress, while during the times of dryness, there is much more progress than when we were joyful. We observe that during the weeks of dryness we have advanced. We normally think that if every day were dry and suffering, we would fall. But when we compare this with our experience, we see that, on the contrary, it was when we felt weak that we advanced. When we are happy, there is not much progress. When the wind is strong and favorable, will it help us develop our muscles? No, our muscles become stronger and stronger during contrary winds. But please remember that for ordinary believers, there is no such thing as so-called up and down spiritual experiences. Our growth is absolutely dependent on the way we exercise our will. When we are dry and exercise our will to say, "I *will* advance," we will advance. Unfortunately, the eyes of many believers are set only on the matter of joy; they think that this is the peak of spiritual experiences. Little do they realize that there is real spiritual progress only when they exercise their will to advance.

C. Overcoming the Environment

If you can overcome the feeling of dryness, you can overcome your environment. The feeling of dryness is the most difficult to overcome. If you can overcome this feeling, you surely will overcome your environment. The environment that is closest to a Christian is his emotion. Only by overcoming your emotion can you overcome other things. If you exercise your will to say, "I *will* read the Bible, I *will* pray, and I *will* testify," even though you are living a dry and parched life, you will find that you can overcome all kinds of environments, no matter how great they may be. I will say frankly that those who have not overcome their environment have not overcome their emotion. Those who would overcome their environment must first overcome their own emotions.

D. Living by Faith

The duration of joy becomes shorter, while the duration of dryness becomes longer. The degree of joy is less, while the degree of dryness becomes more. The end result is that at a certain point, the two will meet. They will be like two streams merging into one; there will not be any distinction between them anymore. At the beginning, the joy becomes shorter and less intense, and the dryness becomes longer and more intense. But in the end, we cannot tell the difference between our joy and our dryness anymore. The reason God is leading us this way is to show us that there will eventually be no difference between the two. In other words, our joy and our dryness will be completely merged as one. Today God has no intention other than having the just live by faith. The just do not live by emotions. Therefore, no matter how we feel in our emotions, they will not bring us anything. Some believers have to go through God's training ten or twenty times until they do not exercise the strength of their emotion. God's training causes the dryness to increase more and the duration to become longer, in order to bring these ones to the point where they will live by faith.

If a man is not saved, we have nothing to say about him. But if he is saved, his experience will surely be one in which the times of dryness become longer, while the times of joy become shorter. His plain days will become more, and his joyous days will become less. God will point out to him what his goal is. Many Christians are living a dry life. Of all the days in a year, he may only experience three to five days of joy. Some may even go through three to five years in dryness, without any joy at all. If you have never been trained, you will see in that day that your emotional strength is useless because the just live by faith.

Finally, if you live by faith, you will be able to live a joyful life in the driest hour and live the driest life in a joyful way. These words seem to be contradictory, but it is a reality in the spiritual life. God is leading you to live such a life by faith.

What is it to live by faith? It is what the three Hebrew men Shadrach, Meshach, and Abed-nego said to Nebuchadnezzar: "Our God...will deliver us out of your hand, O king. But if He does not...we will not serve your gods nor worship the golden image that you have set up" (Dan. 3:17-18). They were saying even if God did not save them, they still would not change. This is to live by faith. Christians today are strongly inclined toward a life in the emotion. Whenever God takes away their feeling of joy, they have nothing left. But God says that we should live by faith and not by feelings. In a few years, we will see that joy and dryness are the same, and neither joy nor dryness can affect us anymore. We will live the same in dryness or in joy. We do not have to live like those whose vessel is small and who are easily satisfied.

When they are happy, they dance in their rooms. When they are dry, they wet the wall with tears. If we live by faith, we will not be affected by either of the two. This does not mean we are insensitive; we do have feelings of joy and dryness. But these outward feelings will not affect us inwardly. (This article covers the joy experienced by the outward man; it does not cover the joy that the inward man enjoys in the Lord. The latter is deep and unshakable. But this deep and unshakable joy can only be enjoyed by us after we can fully control the outward joy.)

CHAPTER TWELVE

LIVING BY FAITH AND
THE COURSE OF ENTERING INTO A TRUTH

Scripture Reading: Heb. 10:38

Two weeks ago I read many verses concerning living by faith. Today I will quote only one verse. Today I will continue with the matter of living by faith, which we began about two weeks ago. We have covered what it is to live by faith and will not repeat it today. However, we have to add a few words to the last message before we can go on with today's subject. What I will speak on is not in any particular order, but will be miscellaneous points, a little here and a little there.

Two weeks ago I mentioned the "wave-like" living of a believer, in which he fluctuates between joy and dryness. For these people, their life goes up and down all the time. After the meeting, some brothers asked me concerning the matter of intensity. They did not understand why the intensity of joy would become less and less, and the intensity of dryness would become more and more, but that in the end there would be no more difference between the two. Concerning this point, I must add a few words today. We use the word *intensity* with a special meaning. On the one hand, there is the real intensity; on the other hand, there is the intensity in the emotion. The intensity of joy that I mentioned last time refers to the intensity of feeling. That intensity becomes less and less. What is real is just the opposite; the intensity of what is real increases. Concerning dryness, the process is the same: in reality it increases, while the feeling decreases. The joy that I mentioned the other day refers to the feeling of joy, which in intensity becomes less and less. The dryness which I mentioned refers to the reality of dryness, which increases in intensity. As far as duration is concerned, the period of joy becomes shorter, while the period of dryness becomes longer. In feeling, the intensity of joy becomes less and less, and in reality, the intensity of dryness becomes more and more. In the end, one feels neither joyful nor dry.

Why are our feelings unreliable? They are unreliable because the God we trust has not changed, the work of the Lord has not changed, and the work of the Holy Spirit has not changed. No matter what your feelings are, they will not affect these things. This was all I said last time. This was only one of the reasons. I will give another reason today. The things on God's side have not changed. The question is whether or not the things within us have changed.

For example, we may have lost all taste for reading the Bible, we may not pray well, and we may feel that we do not have power in our work. We are not as excited as before, and we think that we have fallen. But my question is what is our motive? If our motive has changed, I have nothing to say because we have indeed fallen. But if our motive has not changed, we have not fallen. If our heart is still right, all we have to do is live by faith; we do not have to worry about our feelings.

Once Mr. Hudson Taylor came to Mr. Frost, who was his co-worker of many years, and said, "I am very distressed. I am not the same as when I first came to China. When I first came to China, my soul burned when I saw men who were not saved. I prayed earnestly day and night for God to send men from England and America. For so many years, I loved men's souls, and prayed earnestly, and worked diligently. But there is one thing which is gone: I have lost the initial feeling of excitement; I have fallen. What should I do?" When Mr. Frost heard this, he thought, "This is terrible. Mr. Taylor is the leader of the China Inland Mission. If he has fallen, it is indeed terrible." So he went and prayed for about two weeks. He prayed that God would show him the way to help Mr. Taylor. One day God showed him the clear way. He went to Mr. Taylor and asked him, "Did you consecrate yourself to God when you left England to come to China?" Mr. Taylor said, "Yes, of course I consecrated myself to God." Mr. Frost then asked, "Have you ever taken anything that you consecrated back, during the past years?" He answered, "No." "Has your love for souls diminished?" He answered again, "No." "Has your love for the Lord changed?" The answer was again "No." "Have you become worldly?" "No." "Have you decreased your work in saving souls?" "No." Mr. Frost then said, "If you have all these things, why should you care about your feelings? What can the feelings do?" This apparent failure of Mr. Taylor taught Mr. Frost a lesson that we should not care about our feelings as long as the intention of the heart is right.

It does not matter if we feel we do not like reading the Bible or that we do not find any interest in it. The thing that matters is our motive. Do we have the intention to read the Bible? It does not matter if we feel dull after praying three or five sentences. The thing that matters is whether or not you want to pray. If we did not want to pray, why are we kneeling down? It is one thing for us to feel that it is a good thing to pray; it is another thing for us to want to pray.

Perhaps in testifying to others, we feel terrible after saying a few words. Whether or not we love to testify is one thing; whether or not we have the intention to testify is another. Has our heart for testifying to others changed? Have we loved the world? Has our love for God changed? If our motive has not changed, it does not matter that we feel this way or that way. Please remember clearly that the fluctuating life is something that occurs only in our feelings. Within us, there is only one line; it is neither high nor low. Real failure occurs only when our inward being has changed or when our motive has changed. If our motive has changed, then indeed we are fallen and degraded. After this, if we rise again, it will be a real rising. If we do not rise up, then we have not risen yet; this is not like what is ordinarily referred to as highs and lows, or fluctuations in life.

Now I will speak on living by faith, and what it is like in our spiritual experience. Many Christians still consider it a big problem in their spiritual experience when they find it difficult to deal with the so-called high and low times. For example, when they first hear a new truth, they become very happy. But after two or three days or two or three months, the truth seems to be lost. It seems as if what they received the first time is now all gone and lost, and they consider this a great pity. For this reason, many good brothers have asked what is the proper course of our spiritual experience. In other words, they want to know how they can spiritually advance and progress. This is what I am going to speak about.

Suppose one first hears a truth, such as how to overcome his temper or his rashness, or the truth of Romans 6:6, about the crucifixion of the old man by the Lord's death for the annulling of the body of sin, so that one will no longer be a slave to sin. As a result of hearing this, he becomes happy. He goes home and tells others that from now on, he will no longer lose his temper, for he has received an overcoming truth. He seems to have reached the top of a mountain. He may think that he has reached the peak experience. If he is a husband, he may go home to find his wife doing this and that thing wrong. The first two times, he may hold back his temper. But in the end, he will not be able to hold it back anymore. Now he is bewildered. He thought he understood the truth and would never lose his temper again. But he lost his temper again. Does this mean the truth is unreliable? At such times the environment seems to have made a hole in his boat of truth; all the truth seems to have drained away. Such a person may ask God once more to apply His Word in him so that he will be able to overcome once again. The next time he encounters some frustrating thing, he tries to hold back again. He does this until he can hold back no longer, and he falls again. He cannot understand why the truth that gave him so much joy is all gone. Such trials become more and more severe, and he might think that Romans 6:6 does not work in him anymore; then he becomes disappointed. At such times he sees no light at all; everything is in darkness. When he is standing on the mountaintop, he seems to be able to talk about everything. But now he no longer thinks that those truths are the sword of the Spirit; they seem to be weapons of reed and are completely powerless when he holds them in his hand.

What does this all mean? This is like coming down from the mountaintop and entering into a tunnel. Suppose that there are three mountains. Through the second mountain there is a tunnel. When you think you have the experience of the first mountain, God will bring you down to the plain and put you in an environment in which everything is dark. You will enter the tunnel of the second mountain. After a while, God will lead you out of the tunnel, and you will again experience the joy of the first mountain. But then, you will be on the third mountain. The law of spiritual progress is to go from mountaintops to tunnels and from tunnels to mountaintops. Every time you hear a truth, you will feel that you have obtained it. For example, I may speak on the Lord's teaching on the mount in Matthew 5 to 7, which covers the conduct of Christians. After you hear and receive it, you may think you have reached the peak and are above the world. But you have to remember that this truth is not yours. You only feel this way. In God's eyes you have not attained yet. God has prepared an excellent way; He takes you from a mountaintop down to a plain, and He puts you in your family, your school, your hospital, or in other environments. He puts you in a very dark place, so that you must undergo trials. He brings you down from your idealistic peak experience into a dark tunnel.

All the teachings, truths, and feelings which you received the first time will go with you into the tunnel. Then you will say to God, "God, I cannot lay hold of Your truth. May the truth lay hold of me." When you hear a truth for the first time, you think that it is yours and that you have laid hold of much of the truth. You try your best to lay hold of it, understand it, and practice it. After you make up your mind to do this, God will test you by putting you in many different environments like your family or school. He will permit your family members to disturb you, your colleagues to trouble you, and many other events to surround you. At that time you will see that the truth you once held onto has become like a reed; it seems that it has flown away. You feel that your weapons have been confiscated and everything is lost. You will think that Romans 6:6 cannot be applied to you and slowly lose your grip on the truth. In the end, you give up altogether. This opens the opportunity for God to lay hold of you with His truth. Do not think that this kind of tunnel experience will last for two or three days or for three to five months. Sometimes it lasts for three to five years. At least it is possible for it to last for a year or two.

While you are in such trials, you might think that all is lost. After one or two days, one or two months, or even one or two years, you will not remember the truth anymore, and your hand will lose its grip. Then God will remind you of the truth you once heard, the truth which once gave you an exciting mountaintop experience. Then a small voice may say, "Does not Romans 6:6 say that our old man has been crucified with the Lord, and that the body of sin is annulled, that we should no longer serve sin as slaves?" By then, God will bring you to the point where you can believe. At first you may wonder, "Is this real? Perhaps I have not received it. Perhaps I do not yet understand." You dare not be as bold as the first time and try to act calmly as if nothing has happened. But the same word comes back and reminds you again. Then God will remind you little by little that this is God's Word. You will respond, "Although I still fail, God's Word is sure." Now you find that you can believe. You have come out of the tunnel of the second mountain and have come to the third peak. This will not give you the same feeling you had at the first peak. Without the experience of the tunnel, you cannot have the experience of the third peak. The darkness is past, but trials and difficulties are still there. Nevertheless, you have overcome. The truth you acquire this time is really yours. The truth you received at the first peak was only in your feeling. This is why God disarms your self-confidence at the first peak. He is delivering you from a life of feelings into the realm of living by faith.

The order of receiving any truth from God is this: first He conveys the truth to you through His servant, through some books, or He may give you the understanding directly through reading the Bible. After He gives you the truth, He will immediately begin working and create a sense of need for this truth in you. He will cause something to happen in your environment or work through other things. You will find that unless you experience the deliverance of this special truth, you will not be able to get through. In the beginning, you may think that the truth you understand can save you.

Only when you are put in a trial do you realize that the truth is not yours. After this, you gradually forget this truth. But in your hour of darkness and forgetfulness, the Lord begins to work. Without realizing it, He begins to constitute you with the truth. By the time you come out of the tunnel, you will rediscover that the truth which you forgot in your dark hours has now become ours.

Many believers think that great joy and excitement mean power. But I have to tell you that excitement in one's feelings is actually a hindrance to a life of faith. God has to strip you of everything you have received through your feeling, until only God and His Word remain. He causes you to believe in a calm way; there is no feeling, no excitement. You believe "coldly." When you do that, you are brought up to the mountaintop again. There is joy again, but the joy is different from the first experience of joy. The first experience is groundless, but this joy has a basis. This time God causes you to experience the real victory, not like the previous idealistic victory, because you have passed through the tunnel experience.

Please remember that every time a believer wants to acquire some spiritual experience, he has to first pass through the test of the tunnel before he can really acquire anything. When you acquire a new truth, you are very happy. But you must be careful; immediately after this there is a tunnel waiting for you. If you do not realize this fact and instead doubt the reliability of God's Word, you will be in danger. Because many Christians do not know this principle, they stay inside the tunnel and never come out. God's goal is to remove your outward feelings and your outward crutches, so that His Word will take hold of you and so that you will be empowered through faith. Brothers, before you acquire a spiritual truth, you must always go through the tunnel experience. The feeling on the first peak is not trustworthy. Only after you have gone through the tunnel experience can the truth be yours. This is true with any kind of truth.

At first, we hear a truth and receive it. This is where the teachers come in. They share the truth with us. But we must not think that just because we have heard and understood

it, that it is ours. God has to bring us down from the peak to
the plain and into the tunnel before we can be on the third
peak again. At that time the truth will be ours. There is a particular danger with the preachers. When they reach the first
peak, they think they have acquired something, and they
blow their trumpet to tell others about it. Those who hear
also think that they have acquired the truth. But when they
are brought by God to the plain and into the tunnel, they will
think that what they heard was wrong. The mistake is
with the preachers themselves. When they are on the first
peak, they need not be hasty in telling others anything, for
everything will surely go into the tunnel. The length of time
in the tunnel is not certain; it can be long or short. Only after
they have come out of the tunnel will the truth be theirs.
After they have gone through the tunnel experience, they will
realize what that truth really means. God leads us this way in
order to show us that the just live by faith and not by feeling.
When we are brought into the tunnel, we realize that the
only thing that will bring us through is the Word of God. Only
God's Word counts; feelings do not count. After we pass
through the tunnel experience, the truth will be ours. When
we are brought into the tunnel by God, we think that we have
lost all the truth. Actually, God is turning the truth that we
have received in our feelings into real experience through the
test of the tunnel. In other words, when we are in the tunnel
we acquire the truth in a real way.

Let me now relate to you a story to illustrate this matter.
I have a friend who is a very good poet. One day he went to
a potter to watch how porcelain ware is made. He saw many
people making many vases out of mud, smoothing them out,
and painting flowers and letters on them. Finally, the vases
were burned in the furnace. He thought of the pain the
vases had to go through and wondered if the burning was necessary. A vase that has not gone through the fire looks the
same outwardly as a vase that has gone through the fire. But
inwardly they are very different. A vase that has passed
through the fire can hold water with flowers. A vase that has
not passed through the fire dissolves once water is poured
into it. There must be the burning. He noticed that of the

numerous vases that went into the furnace, only about one-third would come out of the fire undamaged. He was touched by this, and he went home and wrote a poem based on Peter's word about the "fiery ordeal" (1 Pet. 4:12). In the poem he metaphorically described himself as a vase, upon which were painted flowers and letters and colors. It was beautiful, yet it could not stand the touch of a finger or the splash of water. Unless he went through the fire, nothing would be solid or firm. There was no choice but to enter the furnace. Within the furnace, there was the sound of crying and murmuring. But he had to suffer this before he could possess the lasting beauty. When the time came, he emerged out of the furnace. Then there was not only outward beauty, but an inward firmness. All the pictures and letters had firmly become one with him; they belonged to him and could not be erased or washed away anymore. Now he could be presented before anyone, even before a king.

Our experience of acquiring the truth is similar to the experience of the vase. When the flowers and letters are first painted, we think everything is fine. But we cannot stand any touching and are destroyed by any washing. The truth is not ours; we only understand it in our mind and are excited in our feeling. We rejoice over it a little too soon. We have to remember that every time we go through a test, it is to help us to possess the truth that we have just heard. Suppose we have just heard the truth concerning patience. A test will come to make us impatient. The test we will face will put us in exactly the opposite place of the truth we received in our feeling. God wants to put us through the burning of the furnace. Many people go into the furnace and never come out again. But if we go through the fire and come out again, what we have acquired will be firm. Then we will be on the mountaintop once again. The truth which we received before is unusable; but the truth we now have is usable. The sword which we acquired before could not be used to fight; the sword we now have, can. What we had before was only a nice outward appearance; what we now have within is something solid. Previously, we were in the realm of the mind and the emotion; now we have really acquired something.

When we hear a new truth, we go home rejoicing. But what follows are the trials. We must pass through the fire. Here lies the difference between faithful ones and unfaithful ones. It is not enough just to put some nice colors on a vase to make it look nice outwardly. It must go through the fire and come out of the fire before it can be useful. What we receive in our feeling is of no use before God. We have to go through the fire and lose every outward thing before we will receive something real. When we receive a new truth and feel very happy about it, we must not think that we have the truth already. In the tunnel everything is dark; there is no light at all. But we should not think that we have lost the truth we have received initially. We have to realize that this is the time we are actually acquiring the truth. God's goal is to remove us from a life in the emotions and teach us to live by faith. There is only one principle: the just shall live by faith and not by feelings. With every spiritual experience the principle is the same: first there is the mountaintop feeling of joy, then there is the experience of the tunnel, and then another mountaintop joy that is genuine. After this, what we have obtained is real.

Why does God always give us a mountaintop feeling of joy at the beginning of our spiritual experience? God has His intention for doing this. If we do not have a taste of the truth, we will not receive it. Madame Guyon said that God allows us to have a taste of the joy of every new truth, so that we will not want to lose it even when we are in the tunnel. When we pass the test and come out of the tunnel, we will have a full taste of the joy of that truth. First we have a foretaste. After the trial we come into the full and unrestricted enjoyment.

Now we see the proper course of a Christian path. We cannot possess any truth without going through the test of the tunnel. Faith is the principle because feelings are unreliable. God takes away our feelings so that we can have the opportunity of trusting in Him. If our feelings are not removed, we will not trust in God.

Some brothers have asked, "Why is the truth that we think we received in the first peak, the truth we received in our feelings, not trustworthy? Why do we have to pass through the experience of the tunnel before it becomes trustworthy? What does this have to do with our feelings?" The reason is that when we receive the mountaintop feeling of joy concerning a certain truth, we think we have everything and everything is ours. Actually, we still have nothing. God puts us in a tunnel so that the truth can become really ours. When we enter the tunnel, everything is dark, and there is no support anywhere. It seems as if God's Word has failed, and we do not understand why. It seems that God's Word, promises, and facts are all the same and ineffectual. It seems that our feelings have failed us, and according to our feelings, everything is lost. After a while, the truth comes back to look for us. Even though circumstantially we do not feel anything, the truth seems more real and is easier for us to believe. God is delivering us from what we think we have and understand according to our feeling, so that we can actually possess and understand these things. Mr. Andrew Murray once said that the Holy Spirit explains the Word of God to us. I will add a word: only the Holy Spirit can explain God's Word to us. For example, every evening we have our Bible study. Even though we have read and expounded every verse, this does not count; we must forget about these things and allow them to fail inside the tunnel before there can be the beginning of faith. The Holy Spirit must explain the same thing to us a second time. Whatever we think we understand, we understand only in our feelings. We must pass through the tunnel. Only the experience we gain in the tunnel is real. This is the principle of faith.

SECTION THREE

EXPERIENCE

Chapter Thirteen

THE TWO NATURES—
A TALK WITH YOUNG BELIEVERS

A great number of people who have believed in the Lord Jesus as their Savior have discovered a new experience soon after they have believed: in their hearts it seems that there are two natures. These two natures are incompatible with each other. Of the two natures, one is evil and the other is good. Sometimes, when the good nature gains the upper hand, a person becomes very loving, patient, good, and meek. Sometimes, when the evil nature prevails, the person becomes very jealous, ill-tempered, wicked, and stubborn. Those believers who are under this kind of condition experience sudden ups and downs in their life. Sometimes, their spiritual condition seems to be on the mountaintop; at other times, it seems to be in the deep valley. This kind of spiritual life is also like the waves of the sea, at times high and at times low. Believers under this kind of condition are bewildered! Why is there the joy? Why is there the sorrow? Why do we sometimes love a certain person that much and have the ability to tolerate so much of others' ridicule? Why at other times are we so void of love and so impatient? When such a person is at his spiritual peak, he experiences unspeakable joy and peace. When he is spiritually low, he is filled with sorrow and depression. Before such a person believed in the Lord, he did not have much feeling even when he sinned. But now it is very different. He may speak a wrong word or commit a wrong act by accident. Formerly, these things would have been considered trivial, and the conscience would not have been bothered at all. But now, he falls into much *self-condemnation*. Although no one condemns him, he rebukes himself for doing these things.

Such self-condemnation is quite unbearable. It causes the believer to feel ashamed and embarrassed, to feel guilty and condemned. Only after he finds out that the Lord has fully forgiven his sins and he has recovered his spiritual joy can he feel happy again. However, this kind of happiness does not last long. Those believers who remain on this level of life soon find themselves caused to stumble again and their previous joy once more lost! Soon after, they find themselves committing the same sin they committed before! It seems so natural to fall into sin. It is as if a power from within has *overpowered* them in an instant; they are led uncontrollably to speak the wrong words and do the wrong things. Under such a condition, the believers invariably become penitent. They invariably make many vows and resolutions before the Lord. They set up for themselves many ordinances to bind themselves, in the hope that they will not commit the same error again. At the same time, they ask for the cleansing of the Lord's blood afresh and seek for another filling of the Holy Spirit by the Lord. After this, they seem quite satisfied and think that their last sin is behind them, that from now on they are on their way to holiness. However, the fact always turns out contrary to their wish. Soon, perhaps a few days later, they fail again! Once more they fall into deep remorse, bemoaning their own failure and feeling sorrowful at heart; their hopes for holiness have been dashed. All their resolutions and regulations cannot help them. Although they may receive the Lord's forgiveness after this, it becomes difficult for them to believe that they can keep themselves from sinning again. Although they still pray that the Lord would keep them, their heart is full of doubts. They begin to wonder if the Lord can really keep them from sin.

Young believers frequently fall into this kind of experience. Almost daily they come under self-condemnation and sorrow. Sometimes they may condemn themselves several times a day or even several dozen times a day. Such a life of wandering in the wilderness causes them to doubt even their own regeneration. Does not the Scripture say, "He cannot sin, because he has been begotten of God" (1 John 3:9)? They think that if they always sin, it probably means that they are not yet regenerated! The despondency and disappointment at such times are difficult to express even with their tears.

Since these ones have experienced much failure, they make up their mind to be on the alert, to resolve to fight the last battle against the indwelling sin. They remind themselves to watch out for their former weaknesses. They try purposely to improve themselves in areas where they constantly failed before. They resolve as best they can to put off "the sin which so easily entangles us" (Heb. 12:1). This of course affords them much help in their outward conduct. Yet the inward activities of sin continue as before; there is no quelling of its energy. In the end, they fail again. Consider the example of the temper. After a believer realizes that his besetting sin is his quick temper, he will try to control himself in everything. This may work with lesser irritations; it may work in one or two temptations. However, though he may hold back his temper temporarily, further irritations from others will cause his temper to break loose. He may succeed a few times, but as soon as he becomes a little careless, he loses his temper again. At the time of the temptation, he may experience much conflict in his heart. On the one hand, he thinks that he should not lose his temper and should be gentle. On the other hand, he considers the unreasonableness and offense of the other party, and he feels it necessary to vindicate himself by punishing such behavior. This kind of conflict is found commonly among believers. Unfortunately, the result is often failure rather than victory. Once they exhaust their patience, they fail again. A genuinely regenerated person often goes through this kind of experience at the beginning of his Christian life. We do not know how many tears are shed because of defeat in this conflict!

My dear brothers, do you have the experiences we have mentioned? Do you want to know the reason for them? Do you want to overcome? May the Lord bless what we are discussing today so that we will learn to grow in His grace.

Before we speak of our present condition, we should first understand the kind of person we were before we believed in the Lord. After that, we will speak of our condition after we believed in the Lord. We know that we are persons made up of three parts—the spirit, the soul, and the body. The *spirit* is the organ with which we fellowship with God. Animals have no spirit. Hence, they can never worship God. The *soul* is the seat of our personality. Our will, mind, emotion, and sentiments are all functions of the soul. The *body* is our outward shell. Although man has become fallen, he still possesses these three parts. After man is regenerated, he still has the same three parts. When God created man, He created him with a self-consciousness; man was a living creature with consciousness. He had a spirit. Hence, he was different from other lower kinds of creatures. He had a soul. Hence, he was different from the angels of light, who are purely spirits. The center of man was his spirit; it controlled his whole being. It controlled his soul and his body. Man was living totally for God; the emotions of his soul and the demands of his body were all headed up by his spirit, and they were for glorifying God and worshipping God.

But alas, man fell! This fall did not annul any of the three elements in man. However, the order of these three elements has been upset. The condition in the garden of Eden shows us clearly that mankind rebelled against God; his love for God ceased, and he declared his independence from God. Genesis 3:6 says, "And when the woman saw that the tree was good for food [this was the lust of the body, which comes first] and that it was pleasant to the eyes, and a tree to be desired [this was the love of the emotion in the soul, which comes next] to make one wise [this was Satan's suggestion, 'And ye shall be as gods, knowing' (3:5); this was the spirit rejecting God, and man satisfying the cravings of the soul and the body; this comes last]." In this way, man fell, and his spirit, soul, and body were all affected. The spirit became subject to the soul, and the soul was controlled by its many senses. The body developed many abnormal cravings and lusts, which enticed the soul. Originally, the spirit took the lead. Now the body takes the lead to satisfy its lusts. In the Bible, this lust of the body is called the flesh. From this time on, man became flesh (Gen. 6:3). This *flesh* is now man's *nature* after he sinned; it is now his natural constitution. Our nature is the life principle or constitution that directs our whole being.

Since the time of Adam, everyone born of woman bears this sinful nature; all of them are of the flesh. After understanding the origin of the flesh and how the flesh is just our sinful nature, we can now consider the character of this flesh. We cannot expect this flesh to improve. Human nature is hard to change. In fact, it will not change. The Lord Jesus said, "That which is born of the flesh is flesh." We should focus on the word "is." That which is born of the flesh is flesh. No matter how much a person reforms, improves, and cultivates himself, the flesh is *still* the flesh. No matter how much a person tries to perform charitable, benevolent acts, send relief aid, love others, or serve, he is *still* the flesh. Even if he can do all these things, he is still the flesh. "That which is born of the flesh is flesh." Since it is the flesh that is born, it will be the flesh that will result. No man on earth can change his flesh. Neither *can God in heaven* change man's flesh, that is, man's nature.

Since God saw that it was impossible to mend, improve, or change man's sinful nature, He brought in the present wonderful way of redemption. We know that the Lord Jesus died for us on the cross at Golgotha. We also know that when we believe in Him and receive Him as our Savior, we *are* saved. But why does God deliver us from death to life once we believe in His Son's name? If this believing does not involve an *exchange* in our life, which is different from a mere *change,* will not God be delivering a man who is still full of sin into heaven? There must surely be a profound message here.

After we have believed in the Lord Jesus, God does not leave us to walk according to the old sinful nature, that is, the flesh. He sentenced the Lord Jesus to death because He intended, on the one hand, that the Lord become sin for us, and on the other hand, that the old Adamic creation be crucified with Him, so that He could give us a new life. When we believed in the Lord Jesus as our Savior, God gave us this new life with its new nature. "Through these you might become partakers of the divine nature, having escaped the corruption which is in the world by lust" (2 Pet. 1:4). At the time we believed, He dispensed into us His own life, the life of God, with the nature of God. This nature is entirely new; it is totally different from our old sinful nature. This nature does not come from an improvement of our old nature. This mysterious transaction took place at the instant we believed in the Lord Jesus as our Savior. This is regeneration, which is to be born from above and to receive God's life and nature. This regeneration is not something that man feels. Rather, it is the work of God's Holy Spirit in our spirit, recovering our spirit's lost position and installing God's life in our spirit. "The wind blows where it wills, and you hear the sound of it, but you do not know where it comes from and where it goes; so is everyone who is born of the Spirit" (John 3:8). *All* those who have genuinely believed in the Lord Jesus have the Holy Spirit working in them in this way. Those who believe only with their mouth or their head are not regenerated. All those who have believed with their heart are saved (Rom. 10:9) and are surely regenerated.

Now, *two natures* emerge in a believer. One is the sinful nature, the flesh, which is the nature of old Adam. The other is the spiritual life, the "new spirit," which bears God's nature. Brothers, you have believed in the Lord Jesus, and you know that you are saved. For this reason, you are regenerated already. You should now know that there are *two* natures within you. These two natures are the cause of your numerous conflicts. The reason you fluctuate up and down and alternate between victory and defeat is that two natures are exercising their influence over you. These two natures are the key to the riddle of your life of struggling.

For a young believer to have such experiences of inward conflict and condemnation *proves* that he is regenerated. An unregenerated person is still dead in sin. Although he may at times be condemned in his conscience, such feeling is very ill-defined. Without the new nature, it is obvious that a person will not experience the conflict between the new nature and the old.

The Bible clearly describes this conflict between the new nature and the old. In Romans 7, Paul vividly portrayed this kind of life of conflict through his own experience. He said, "For what I work out, I do not acknowledge; for what I will, this I do not practice; but what I hate, this I do" (v. 15). This is doing what he does desire to do. Since the new nature is holy, when a person fails, he feels repentant and condemns himself, and he pleads for the sin-cleansing blood. Brothers, by now, you should understand the reason for your conflicting experiences. This kind of conflict shows most assuredly that you are regenerated.

The most crucial question now is: how can we overcome? In other words, how can we reject the power and work of the old nature, and walk according to the aspirations of the new nature, and thus please the Lord? Let us read three verses:

"But they who are of Christ Jesus have crucified the flesh with its passions and its lusts" (Gal. 5:24).

"If we live by the Spirit, let us also walk by the Spirit"; "But I say, Walk by the Spirit and you shall by no means fulfill the lust of the flesh" (vv. 25, 16).

These three verses tell us two ways to overcome the flesh, that is, the sinful nature, the old nature, and the old Adamic nature. Actually, the two ways are merely two aspects, or two phases, of one way. The cross and the Holy Spirit are the unique way to overcome the sinful nature. Other than this way, any human resolutions, determinations, or vows to charity are destined for failure.

We have seen that all our failures are caused by the tenaciousness of the sinful nature; we sink to such a low condition because of it. Hence, whether or not we will overcome depends on whether or not we are able to deal with this sinful nature, which is the flesh. Thank God that though we are helpless, He has the way. He has prepared a way for us on the cross. When the Lord Jesus was crucified on the cross, not only did He die for us, but He crucified our flesh *with Him* on the cross. Hence, all those who belong to Christ Jesus and are regenerated have their flesh crucified. When He died on the cross, our flesh was crucified there as well. Both the substitutional death and the identifying death have been accomplished by the Lord Jesus. Both are *fully accomplished.* Formerly, we believed in His substitutional death and were regenerated. Now, in the same way, we believe that our flesh is crucified with Him, and we are brought into the experience of the death of the flesh.

We know that the flesh is always the flesh. This is why God gave us a new life and a new nature. But what shall we do with the flesh? Since God considered it hopeless and impossible, He decided to terminate it, that is, to put it to death. There is no better way than to cause the flesh to die. Hence, "they who are of Christ Jesus have crucified the flesh with its passions and its lusts." This puts the flesh to death. This is what the Lord Jesus has accomplished; He has accomplished it already. By crucifying our flesh with Him, it becomes possible now for us to put to death the sinful nature. This has been accomplished without any effort of our own.

How can this co-crucifixion become our experience? We have said that the way is by faith. Romans 6:11 says, "So also you, *reckon* yourselves to be dead to sin." Sin here refers to the sinful nature which is the flesh. By ourselves, we cannot cause the flesh to die. The only way is by reckoning. Reckoning is an exercise of our will and our faith. This means that in our daily life, we should adopt the attitude that we are dead to the flesh, that we believe in God's word, and that we consider all God's words to be true. God says that our flesh has been crucified with the Lord Jesus; I believe that my flesh is indeed crucified. On the one hand, we believe that we are dead. On the other hand, we adopt the attitude that we are truly dead. If we do this, we will have the genuine *experience* of dying to sin.

If we reckon this way, we will see the cross freeing us, and the flesh will become powerless. It is true that once we reckon ourselves dead, we will experience instant victory. However, many people experience a gradual deliverance from the power of the flesh. This is either due to their own foolishness or to the lingering of evil spirits. If we persist in faith and if we take the proper attitude in our will, we will eventually overcome. However, this does not mean that henceforth there is no more sinful nature in us and that only the new nature remains. If we say this, we fall into heresy. Not only does this obscure the teaching of the Bible, but it betrays the experience of the saints. Until we are delivered from this body of sin, we will never be free from the "flesh"—the sinful nature—which comes from the body of sin.

Even though we have accepted the work of the cross, the fact that the flesh still exists means that we must continually "walk by the Spirit." Only by doing this, will we "by no means fulfill the lust of the flesh."

The cross is the instrument by which we crucify the flesh. The Holy Spirit is the power by which we keep the flesh from resurrecting. *On the negative side,* we should believe in the co-crucifixion of the cross for the elimination of a life in the flesh. *On the positive side,* we should walk according to the Spirit so that the flesh will have no chance to be rekindled. Many believers experience the resurrection of their flesh because they fail in this one point. Every time we walk contrary to the Holy Spirit, we give opportunity to the flesh to reign. If in everything we walk according to the Spirit, the flesh will not have any opportunity.

A person can read about this way of overcoming the flesh, the sinful nature, from the Bible; he can hear about it from others. But only when he encounters it in his experience will he realize that it is real. I often tell others that they can experience such a matter the minute they believe. Yet for myself, it took me a long time before I experienced it! What does this mean? Many times we merely strive. Although we say that we trust in the cross, thirty percent of the time we trust in ourselves and in our own "reckoning." Many times God allows us to be defeated so that in the end we would realize that nothing is trustworthy in our experience. Even our own "reckoning" with which we "reckon" ourselves dead is of no merit. This is why it is true to say that as soon as we truly reckon, we have the experience of victory, and it is equally true to say that we enter such experience only through a gradual understanding.

Brothers, by now you can understand our two natures and the way to overcome the flesh. While you are reading, you can exercise your faith to reckon yourself dead to sin, and you can pray that the Holy Spirit of the Lord will apply the cross of the Lord Jesus deeply in you, so that you can overcome sin in your experience. After this, you should resolve to walk by the Holy Spirit. Previously, you have failed in your resolution. Now, you should ask the *Holy Spirit to strengthen* your will, so that it will be able to incline itself to the new nature. The will is like a rudder; it can turn the whole ship. However, a rudder that does not work is useless. After the Holy Spirit has strengthened you, you should exercise this will to walk according to the Holy Spirit. Remember that the flesh never disappears; it is always there. If you walk by the Holy Spirit, you will be able to crucify the flesh on the cross continually. Otherwise, the flesh will cause suffering to you. The meaning of walking by the Spirit is to trust in the Holy Spirit in a calm way in everything, so that you will bear the nine-in-one fruit of the Holy Spirit. The Lord will lead you experientially step by step into the mystery of this matter. However, on your part, you should be faithful.

CHAPTER FOURTEEN

HONESTY, DECEPTION, AND SPIRITUAL KNOWLEDGE

Spiritual knowledge is always helpful. It gives us a clearer direction to spiritual progress. Ignorance always leads to mistakes.

Saints go astray because they do not have spiritual knowledge. Satan mainly utilizes the foolishness of the saints to mislead them. The Holy Spirit is not afraid of man having knowledge, spiritual knowledge. The more knowledge a man has, the easier it is for the Spirit to lead him. The devil is the authority of *darkness;* he utilizes darkness, loves darkness, and wants to keep man in darkness. The less knowledge a man has, the easier it is for Satan to deceive him.

There is a misconception among Christians that as long as they are honest they will not be deceived. They think, "My intention is very honest; therefore, I will not be deceived." Little do they realize that mainly honest people are deceived. The saints who are deceived by Satan usually think that they are seeking the truth with a very *honest heart.* They pray, read the Scriptures, fast, and pursue spiritual experiences. Nevertheless, they are still susceptible to deception. They do not realize that Satan can very easily inject an erroneous thought into their minds. They also do not realize that Satan can very easily put a stubborn will in their hearts so that they will become obstinate in their thinking and consider their thoughts as the truth, besides which there is no other truth. They think that since they seek God's gift with an *honest heart,* God will surely keep them from deception. Little do they realize that God has certain conditions for keeping man from deception. If a saint does not cooperate with God by persisting in his opposition to Satan, if he does not ask the Lord for light to discern the real condition of the situation, or if he will not submit to God's words, then God *cannot* keep him. God *did not* promise to keep us unconditionally. On the contrary, we should work together with God. Only then will He keep us.

First, Satan deceives the saints by saying, "You will not be deceived." Those who believe that they will never be deceived will be deceived more frequently and seriously than others. Due to pride, Satan became Satan; he works by causing people to become proud. However, some pride is obvious and some is concealed. (Alas! Sometimes this pride is concealed to such an extent that a person thinks that he can never be deceived and secretly pities others for not having his unusual experiences!) Those who are proud and think that they cannot be deceived should be careful, or they will eventually be deceived.

If we are humble and not self-assuming or stubborn, if we admit that we can easily be deceived, if we single-heartedly seek the Lord so that He would reveal the real condition and true significance behind every matter, and if we wholeheartedly resist the works and wiles of the enemy, we will know if our spiritual experience is from God or from Satan.

We should know that Satan can transform himself into an angel of light and his evil spirits can transform themselves into ministers of *righteousness*. The unusual experiences we have gained may be very good and may help us to go on. They may put a flame in our hearts and give us great joy. We may even speak in tongues, receive healings, dream dreams, hear spiritual sounds, constantly have third-heaven experiences, and know the most mysterious things. Sometimes, we may be affected by a spirit outside of us that makes us feel that Jesus is most precious. In our prayer we may feel that the Lord is in the room and there is no need to pray to God in heaven, and instead we only need to pray to the Lord in the room. However, we must never think that these experiences are from God. It is possible that we may be deceived. Do not think that just because we seek with a very sincere heart, we can never be deceived. An honest heart is not a condition that prevents one from being deceived. There are hundreds of thousands of honest believers who have been deceived. It is difficult to say that we will not also be deceived. For this reason, we should have spiritual knowledge.

We should know the spiritual *law*. God works according to definite principles. If believers *do not know* and walk according to the law of God's work, God *cannot* keep us. The most crucial question for us is: are we *willing to reject* all of our wonderful, unusual experiences if they *are not* from God?

Do not think that we are always willing to reject these experiences. Actually, we find too much unwillingness within our hearts. I am afraid that our hearts love our wonderful experiences too much! Until this matter is resolved, we cannot obtain any knowledge to go on spiritually. After the first step is resolved, we can then look at the second step. Our present attitude should be: if my experience is not from God, I will resist and oppose it. I resist and oppose everything that is from Satan. Before God, I unceasingly ask Him to reveal the *real condition* behind every matter to me. If we do this, God will direct us and enlighten us *in His own time*. Concerning supernatural experiences, unless we have actually *tested* the source of our experience, we should not *lightly believe* in it. Speculation and deduction are totally unreliable in dealing with things in the spiritual realm. If God has not revealed the real condition behind a particular matter to us in our spirit and we have not actually tested whether it is from God, we must not assume that it has been given by God. Unless God gives us the knowledge, we have nothing to believe. Our honest heart cannot keep us from being deceived. If we do not want to be deceived, God must give us the knowledge so that we can understand the real condition behind every matter.

CHAPTER FIFTEEN

CALMNESS OF MIND

5/23/2023

It is very easy for the heart to become cold; it is also extremely difficult for the head to remain calm. We do not have to plan or endeavor. In the twinkling of an eye, when we are just slightly unwatchful, our loving heart toward God and man spontaneously cools down. But it is not so with our head. Many times, the more we think, the more confused we become, and also the more we think, the hotter we become. We lose our calmness because we are agitated. The heart should be hot and the head should be cool. Being calm in our head is to keep from being agitated in our thoughts. Saints who seek for the fullness of life must pay attention to their head. Although a man's thoughts cannot control his life, they do affect his life. If a man is not calm in his head, he will not be calm in his attitude and life. Once a man's head is hot, he cannot control himself. Self-control is the ninth item of the wonderful fruit of the Holy Spirit. Losing self-control is to lose the fragrance of the Holy Spirit which runs through our life. Once our head is agitated, we unconsciously change from the way we normally behave. Under these circumstances, we are tossed to and fro like waves, floating in the air, and unable to control ourselves. Our words, deeds, and conduct are subconsciously affected by the mental agitation in our head; so we begin to act abnormally. Notwithstanding, believers who have suffered this do not realize their loss.

When we are calm, it is easy to discern the agitation of others. But when we are agitated, we may not see our own problem. When we observe the actions, words, and attitude of an agitated person, we may condemn him, saying, "So-and-so is bound by his flesh." Nevertheless, when we are agitated and behave the same way, we may not see our own problem.

This is the difference between being calm and being agitated. If we are calm in our mind, we will have a very clear understanding and accurate evaluation concerning everything; otherwise, we will confuse right with wrong and lose all standards of good and evil.

Not only can we observe this behavior in others; we can see it in ourselves. After we are agitated and changed in our behavior, which results in abnormal conduct and abnormal speech, our anger begins to subside and our head begins to calm down. If we would quietly reflect upon the way we conducted ourselves during our agitation, we would secretly laugh at our previous mistakes. Either we will deeply condemn ourselves or be ashamed of our former conduct and secretly blush. When our head is calm, we will not repeat the same things that we did when our head was hot. If we maintain our calmness, we will not approve of agitated conduct. Nevertheless, we have become agitated many times. When we are agitated, our conduct becomes either sinful or loose. The more we consider, the angrier we become. We burn with fury within and become agitated by the flesh. As a result, we fall into sin. When we are agitated, we often sneer unnaturally, jest, or speak words which contradict our inward feelings. The tide of our thoughts roars, rising and falling. Sometimes we can neither sleep at night nor eat during the day. Sometimes we are joyful; sometimes we are sorrowful. Sometimes we fiercely plod on and labor, or we purposely hold back and drag our feet. None of these phenomena portray our true intention. When everything is over and we sit before the Lord to reflect and examine ourselves under His light, we would often laugh at ourselves and wonder that we have been so soulish!

We all know that the way we behave during times of agitation is wrong. Nevertheless, when we are agitated, we have no power to control ourselves. Since this is the case, we should guard ourselves from agitating things. We should maintain a calmness in our head. If we know that we have been agitated, we should say to ourselves, "I have been agitated. I better not do anything now or I will have another failure." We should resist Satan and stop him from taking advantage of these agitating situations. Learn to be a master

over yourself at such times. Learn to manage the agitation
and subject it to yourself. The first victory will increase your
capacity to have the second victory. If we do not know whether
we are agitated, we should ask ourselves, "Am I speaking,
thinking, and behaving this way because I am agitated?" If so
we should ask the Holy Spirit to strengthen us so that we can
control ourselves. We should control the agitation rather than
being controlled by the agitation.

Agitation is often the instrument that Satan utilizes to
cause saints, first, to commit sin (especially anger) and,
second, to stray from God's will. If by any chance we become
careless in this matter, we bring shame to the Lord's name.
Whenever your thoughts are shaken and your emotions confused, do not forget this. Calmness of head is the condition for
maintaining one's peace. The loss of peace occurs mainly
because your head becomes agitated. Agitation usually results
in the loss of peace. However, it is possible for one to keep his
peace even after he is agitated. When the cross, manifested by
God's word, works deeply within us, causing our spirit and
soul to be divided in experience, we will have the full power to
take charge of the agitation. Even though the environment
and things surrounding the heart may be confused and uncer-
tain, the heart will not be moved, and an inward, calm
serenity will prevail. Though things done in agitation may
sometimes be good, *none* of them are perfect. Having a calm
head is a necessary condition for the Holy Spirit to lead us to
walk according to God's will. When we are agitated, Satan
will have the opportunity to manipulate us and will lead us
off the right track. A calm head will give the Holy Spirit an
opportunity to lead us. The Holy Spirit cannot utilize our con-
fusion; rather, when we are in a calm spirit, He will shine
calm light into our mind so that we may know His will. Even
the most spiritual saint cannot completely avoid agitation;
unless he is on the alert all the time, he is not free from this
danger. Those who follow the Lord soberly must pay attention
to this matter.

Chapter Sixteen

BORROWED SPIRITUAL EXPERIENCE

Experience should be something personal. What you have not experienced cannot be called experience. If scriptural teachings and doctrines are not experienced personally by us, they have nothing to do with us. The teaching remains a teaching, and the doctrine remains a doctrine. Experience is a matter of life; it is not an idea. Mental thoughts can provide man with many beautiful notions. However, only experience can provide man with a well-developed human life.

It is very unfortunate that the believers' mental life is more advanced than their experiential life. In regard to our real spiritual condition as Christians, we do not possess what we think but only what we have experienced. Some Christians have no deep experience in the Lord themselves. They do not have novel ideals or an ideal human life; nevertheless, they are very good imitators. One cannot say that they have no heart for spiritual teachings; on the contrary, they are full of interest in spiritual teachings and are very attentive to them. Their heart very much admires the experience of others in the Lord. Although they do not have much fellowship with the Lord, they appreciate the fellowship that others have with the Lord. Although they do not have a burning love or intimate affection for the Lord, they delight in the expression and words of love by others to the Lord. Although they do not have a strong faith in the Lord that would cause them to pray unceasingly to Him and receive numerous miraculous and wonderful answers to their prayers from God, they wholeheartedly praise and admire this kind of spiritual experience. They end up with many pretensions because their hearts are so drawn to these things.

Before these Christians believed in the Lord and were regenerated, they must have been outgoing, fond of fame, emotional, and greedy for vainglory. After being regenerated and saved, these Christians greatly desire to rapidly advance in their spiritual progress in order that they may be known as spiritual giants and obtain a great name and glory. We cannot say that their whole intention is to gain vainglory and reputation. As a matter of fact, they are not behind others in their spiritual pursuit. However, in the hidden part of their heart, to a greater or lesser extent, there secretly remains the motivation of self-glory. This motive, for the most part, is responsible for their seeking heart and strength. However, few of them fulfill their aspiration.

Spiritual progress is made one step at a time. It is like taking a journey. Those who progress spiritually simply serve the Lord faithfully; they do not take the wrong way; they do not turn back; they are not obstinate, and they obey fully. Therefore, they are able to finish the long journey in the shortest period of time. Those who want to rapidly advance try to double the speed of their progress by their own strength and methods, without realizing that there is no short cut in spiritual progress! As a matter of fact, these believers have more difficulty advancing than believers who are apparently slow. The slow believers apparently miss something, and the hasty ones apparently gain something. Actually, neither kind have gained anything. A slow believer realizes the activity of his sinful nature and his many failures. When these failures repeatedly occur, he loses heart and thinks that he will never attain to maturity in spiritual life and that he can never overcome. This is not entirely correct. It is comparatively easy for God to deal with a slow believer and cause him to go on. However, hasty believers are most difficult for God to deal with. In reality they are as troubled by their flesh as slow believers. Many times they are even more troubled. They fail often, yet their nature makes it hard for them to admit their mistakes and failures before *men*. Their vain hearts are fervent, yet their daily failures make it hard for them to be boastful. When they fail, they grieve over the glory they have lost before man more than the sin they have committed.

Although their "outward hearts" will not admit that they are greedy for vainglory, their "inward hearts" are constantly clinging to vainglory. Because they are vainglorious, they devote their attention to outward appearance, and because they devote their attention to outward appearance, they fall into hypocrisy.

Their flesh and sinful nature often rebel against them and constantly cause them to fall. But this does not make them humble (except when their failures are known by men). Since they have no real spiritual experience and their motive is not pure and right, they *borrow* the spiritual experiences of others and take them as their own. They secretly acquaint themselves with other people's spiritual messages and, at an opportune time, take one or two statements from them in order to gain a reputation for eloquence and spiritual depth. Little do they realize that what they say does not appear to originate from their manner of life! Their words and their living are not compatible with each other! They imitate the intimate talk others have with the Lord and adopt it as their own. Little do they realize that their spirit and expression, while they are talking, do not match their words. They also have a wide collection of quotations from famous saints with observations about the world and seemingly everything. When an opportunity comes, they apply these quotations one by one. Little do they care that their heart inwardly accuses them of their hypocrisy! These believers often hear of many experiences of answered prayer, and they try to manufacture the same kind of experience in order to be admired by others! Little do they realize that their own hearts are doubting if God will answer their prayer. They hear others praise and thank God in their suffering, and they imitate the praises to God by lifting up their voice when in similar suffering. Yet they only have a praising mouth without a praising heart. This is not acceptable to God. Even more frequently, they adopt spiritual words that they hear in the prayers of others, loving thoughts expressed to the Lord from the hearts of others, and the burning enthusiasm for saving souls poured out from the hearts of others. Their failure lies in the fact that even though they pray such words, their hearts do not respond (except for occasional emotional sentiments), and they have no desire for such things.

Sometimes we hear others minister the deep teachings of spiritual life. Because of a preacher's thorough elucidation, we clearly understand in our mind what has been said. At such times there is a great danger that we may think that what we understand is also our experience. Little do we realize that at critical moments, we may still be found unfaithful in following the preacher's teaching and in working together with the Lord. Everything that we have not experienced is not ours. What we understand only belongs to others. We still have nothing!

Borrowed spiritual experience leads to self-pride and haughtiness. It leads us to think that we have reached the very highest realm. We are greedy for vainglory which only corrupts us spiritually. Borrowed spiritual experience cannot help us to advance spiritually; on the contrary, it will be an absolute hindrance to our spiritual advance. Pride and vainglory are sufficient to cause a fatal blow to the saints. It is not worth it to bring loss upon ourselves. On that day when we are before the judgment seat of Christ, all "borrowed things" will be made manifest. Not one false thing will remain covered before the judgment seat. May we be willing to be instructed. May we be more humble and not assume that we already know. Rather, may we be faithful before the Lord to ask ourselves, "Have I attained to this stage yet?"

Chapter Seventeen

ESSENTIALS AND NONESSENTIALS

How do we differentiate between essentials and nonessentials? We often hear God's children say that such and such a teaching in the Bible is essential, and such and such a teaching is nonessential. How do we differentiate between the two? What are essential teachings, and what are nonessential teachings?

If we exercise careful observation, we will find many who consider that questions related to their *own* salvation are essential teachings and questions unrelated to their salvation are nonessential teachings. This is why we often hear people say, "Do I have to obey the Lord in this matter? I do not think this matter is essential because it is not related to my salvation." Even more foolish Christians will ask, "Does this matter have to do with my salvation? If it has to do with my salvation, I will obey it. If not, what difference will it make if I do not obey it? I am saved already!"

Let me ask once more: what is essential and what is nonessential? Some may answer, "The essentials are teachings that have to do with the salvation of the saints, and the nonessentials are teachings concerning God's commandments and His glory! The commandments and glory of God are nonessential because they have nothing to do with the saints' going to heaven and receiving eternal life!" The fact that something is merely a commandment of God and merely related to God's glory is not enough to motivate the saints to obey.

It is a pity that this is the condition of many people today. The saints will only obey and submit if they consider that keeping all of the commandments and obeying all of God's will is necessary in order to be saved. God has said that those who believe in the Lord Jesus have eternal life; therefore, since they have believed and received eternal life, believers think that there is no further need to be concerned with God's other commandments and will. Other than the questions of heaven and hell, nothing moves the saints' hearts anymore. Even God's own glory is something minor to the saints. Unless God makes all of His commandments as conditions for salvation, He cannot expect some saints to obey them. This is because all they hope and plan for is receiving eternal life and going to heaven. Pleasing God and submitting to His will are peripheral issues. How pitiful is this situation!

The saints today are most selfish. Nothing can attract their attention except those things that have to do with their salvation. Is this the standard that God requires? He wants us to obey Him willingly and not by force. He loves to bestow grace to us and give us eternal life once we believe in His Son. Unlike the time of the law, He has not made His commandments as conditions for our salvation. Unfortunately, believers are not willing to be obedient children and walk according to the Father's will. On the contrary, they ask, "Is this something essential, or is it something nonessential?"

We admit that with biblical teachings, some are *more important,* while others are *less important.* But we do not agree that there are essential and nonessential biblical teachings. Would God be so uneconomical as to put meaningless and nonessential teachings, commandments, and doctrines into the Bible? He should know better than we do! The present question is not whether or not a biblical teaching is essential. If it is included in the Bible, it surely is essential. The question is whether or not the saints will honor God's glory and His will. If we consider the Lord Jesus' conduct on earth, our mouths will be shut. He was the Son of God. There was no need for Him to consider the question of His own salvation! Then according to the principle of men today, nothing about Him would have been essential because He did not need to be saved. But how He obeyed God! Even in the smallest matter, He fulfilled all righteousness. He was not like men today who scrupulously bargain with God in questions beyond their salvation.

There is yet another distinction between essential and nonessential. It is a personal distinction. The things that a saint obeys, he considers as essential; the things that he has not followed, but rather disobeyed God in, he considers as nonessential. The difference between essential and nonessential does not lie in the fact that the Bible has said it, but rather in one's own view. Because one has obeyed in a certain matter, he considers the teaching he has obeyed as essential and draws back from other teachings which he has not obeyed.

Alas, now is the time for God's children to be revived. Now is the time for us to be revived to obey God's commandments. May we pay close attention to God's glory and truly care for His will in the same way that Paul declared "all the counsel of God." May we not separate God's Bible into essential and nonessential parts according to our own will. We have to realize that obeying in big matters is indeed obedience. But obeying in small matters is also obedience. Disobeying in big matters is disobedience. Is disobedience in small matters not also disobedience? May we walk according to the teaching of the Bible and take God's glory as our goal in everything that we do in our lives, whether great or small.

One cannot say that eating of the tree of the knowledge of good and evil was a great matter. But since God forbade man to do it, eating of the tree became the source of sin. One little sin drove Adam from the garden of Eden. Was Achan's sin a great one? What he stole was probably not worth that much. But since he disobeyed God, he was punished. Why did Saul lose his kingdom? He did not commit a terrifying sin; he only disobeyed God in a little thing. Did Moses commit a great sin when he was barred from entering Canaan? The Bible says that he was the most humble person on earth. Why did he suffer such punishment from God? It was only because of a small thing. God told him to *command* the rock to flow out water, yet he *hit* the rock twice. Humanly speaking, what kind of sin can this be considered? In men's eyes today, such a matter would be considered nonessential. But *God* never considers any of His commandments to be nonessential. May we henceforth obey God more and more!

CHAPTER EIGHTEEN

BRIBING THE CONSCIENCE

The conscience is God's voice of righteousness within man. It is a part of the spirit, and its function is to rebuke everything that is not of God and against righteousness. It is a prosecutor, and it restrains man from doing anything that falls under its jurisdiction.

Believers are often fearful of their conscience! Those whose hearts are right obey the correction and guidance of the conscience; those whose hearts are not right try to bribe their conscience and silence its accusations. But can the conscience be bribed? The conscience cannot be bribed. After believers have tried their bribe, they think that they no longer need to heed the voice of their conscience. Actually, the voice of their conscience is only confused and drowned out by other voices.

Many times, our conscience tells us clearly through intuition what is God's will, where it lies, and what it requires of us. But we are reluctant in submitting to it! The one thing that the flesh fears the most is the will of God. One can say that the flesh fears nothing other than God's will. Since the mind of the flesh does not like God's decisions, it is naturally unwilling to obey them, and the conscience has to urge a person on. When the urging becomes ineffective, the rebukes of the conscience follow. This feels terrible! If one allows his conscience to work, his heart will become uneasy, and he will feel terrible! This is truly unbearable. In order to avoid the condemnation of the conscience and, at the same time, continue to disobey God's will, one has to bribe the conscience.

In this lies all the mistakes of a believer. He does not seek a solution that will deliver him from the condemnation of the conscience. Rather, he tries to confuse and mix up its voice with other voices in order to minimize its pricking power. But the best way to be free from the condemnation of the conscience is to remove what the conscience condemns and obey God's will in all things. Anything else will cause the believer to offend the Lord even more.

How numerous are the excuses! When believers do not obey God's will, their conscience condemns them. What then can they do? The only thing they can do is to explain, argue, and give reasons and causes for their present disobedience. This is a bribing of the conscience. Believers behave this way because they think that if they can explain the reason for their actions to others and themselves, their disobedience to God's will, in turn, will become His will. Little do they realize that this can never happen. Nevertheless, realizing that the condemnation of their conscience is difficult to bear, they try every means to stop it. If they cannot obey God's will, they appease themselves by giving reasons for their disobedience to God, hoping to blunt the cutting edge of the knife and minimize their own hurt. On the one hand, the conscience condemns. On the other hand, the flesh is unwilling to obey. Consequently, the only solution is to use many reasons and explanations to quell the conscience, telling it that the way they have taken is the right way and that there is no reason for it to continue the condemnation.

There are other ways to bribe the conscience. One of the ways is through labor. If one is unwilling to obey God, he will try to substitute God's will with greater and more numerous works, as if the increased labor can take the place of God's will. Many believers try to suppress the condemnation of the conscience through busy activities. They are afraid to think and afraid to quietly listen to what their conscience is saying. If they listen, they feel uneasy. They are willing to suffer, work, and labor in their mind and bodies apart from God's revealed will. By working in this way, they have no time and are able to ignore the corrections of their conscience with peace. Even if the conscience is able to slip in some unpleasant remarks, they are able to answer on the basis of their work and bribe it into silence. "Are not these works equally important? Are they not equally good? Are they not important? Do they not bear fruit?" When the conscience is repeatedly drowned out by these sounds, it becomes difficult to hear its voice anymore. From this point on, the believers build up a defense and are free to disobey God.

It is very serious to bribe one's conscience. But one bribes his conscience in many of the small things that occur in his daily life. The most common example is the reading of the Bible in the morning. The conscience condemns going to work in the morning without first reading the Bible. However, many believers fail in this matter. If they do not read the Bible, they feel uneasy. But they are unwilling and not interested in reading it. For this reason, they mindlessly open the Bible and read one or two verses, counting that as their reading of the Bible. This silences the voice of their conscience. This bribes the conscience with one or two verses and stops its condemnation.

Are not many prayers offered up in the same way? This is especially true in the case of making supplications for others. If one does not pray for others, he feels condemned in his conscience. Reluctantly, he makes supplications for others by calling their names one by one, like taking roll in a school. This type of reading the Bible and praying for others is not for the purpose of reading and supplication, but for the purpose of silencing the accusation of the conscience. If the conscience did not speak, this type of reading and prayer would have stopped long ago. But since the conscience is diligent, one realizes that he cannot let down at all and instead has to bribe his conscience with half-hearted works.

The same is true of the gospel work among many workers. When some feel emotionally low and physically weak, they become lazy in preaching the gospel. But many times, sinners are placed before them and need to be saved immediately. If these workers remain silent for a long time, the conscience will voice its usual accusation. Under such circumstances, they reluctantly speak a few words about salvation to others in order to bribe their conscience. They think that by speaking, they have fulfilled their duty and that nothing more can be said against them. Whether or not the conscience still accuses them is a secondary question. The serious matter is that believers would even consider answering the interrogation of their conscience with such half-hearted acts. Once they engage in such careless acts, they become self-satisfied and feel that they have not neglected their duties. Alas, how many self-proclaimed "not guilty" verdicts are in fact deceptive! How can these works expect God's blessing? How can teachings that do not touch oneself touch sinners? Those who do not sow in tears will surely not reap in joy.

Shall I mention one more thing? In the matter of material giving, there are more bribes of the believers' conscience. They may be loath to offer, even though they will be accused by their conscience if they do not offer to the Lord. The best way to take care of this dilemma is to offer just a little to bribe the conscience so that the conscience will know that some money has been offered. Since what should be done has been done, there is no more reason for the conscience to nag. Many times, an offering of a few dollars to the poor is not done out of a love for the poor, but to silence and bribe the conscience. Actually, unless an offering results in a painful touch of the heart, a pain of joy to the extent that his flesh feels some kind of pain, the offering cannot be considered as a real offering.

We have mentioned but a few examples. In a believer's daily life, he bribes his conscience in many other things. He either reasons and argues with the conscience or uses other means to substitute for the demand of the conscience. Such acts are too frequent! This explains the fallen and shallow nature of a believer's spiritual life. Brothers, do not think that our knowledge of the Bible is too small and that we do not know God's will in many matters. I will readily admit that this is true. But if our knowledge of the Bible is shallow, this is all the more reason to obey the "inner voice." Undoubtedly, we are still not clear about God's will in many things. But why will we not act on what we *already know*? Bribing the conscience is proof that we know what we ought to do and that we know God's will, but we are unwilling to do it. This is why we bribe the conscience.

Brothers, it is important that we obey God's will faithfully. Before we do this, we must have a sincere *willingness* to do

God's will. Everything else is futile. We are not after success, the world's recommendations, or even peace in our conscience. If our goal is only to secure the peace of our conscience and we fully abide by God's will, we are still bribing our conscience. We must see the greatness and solemnity of God's will. We must obey God's will for the sake of God's will. The voice of the conscience merely shows us where we have left the track of God's will. If, while we live in this world, we do not live for God's will, we are indeed selfish! Are we afraid of the accusation of our conscience more than of our disloyalty to God Himself? We should be afraid of acting contrary to the will of God. Regrettably, we live in this world for our own pleasure. Even when we obey God's will, it is for the purpose of making ourselves feel comfortable! Because disobedience to the will of God results in the accusation of our conscience, the loss of peace and joy, and suffering to our heart, we reluctantly go along with the leading of our conscience, hoping that this will recover our joy. Oh, how selfish this is! This bribes the conscience.

We have to have a fresh evaluation of God's will. We have to exercise a deeper rejection of our self and have a more severe dealing with and deeper hatred for self-deception. If we would give up our act of bribing the conscience and live in God's will day by day, we would find ourselves living in a new realm.

CHAPTER NINETEEN

THE CONDESCENSION OF THE LORD JESUS

Only the One who is the highest can condescend to be the lowest. The whole life of our Lord shows us that He condescended in this way. When we read the four Gospels, we see a condescending life unfold before us. This is one of the reasons that we admire and worship Him. There are many aspects to His condescension, but the most beautiful one is His co-working with His creatures and employing them to be the instruments for His work.

He is the Creator. He creates things out of nothing. As soon as He says something, it is done. His words are absolute and infinite. Behind His words is His mighty power which accomplishes what He says. He does not need any helper or raw material. His authority is sufficient to accomplish everything. The Creator does not need co-workers or instruments.

Yet, how amazing are His acts on the earth! He used the seven loaves and a few fish that the disciples offered Him to feed four thousand. If He could feed four thousand with seven loaves and a few fish, He could have fed them without any loaf or fish by creating the loaves and the fish instead. For Him both ways are equally easy. He could perform miracles, any kind of miracles. For Him, creating something out of nothing and increasing something out of a little is equally easy. But He condescended. He was happy to share His glory and work with His disciples. He wanted to bring His people into the work that He was doing. He did not want to be alone. He did not want to do everything by Himself. He wanted to work together with His people. He desired to see His people participating in His work. He was happy to lead the creatures into the work of the Creator. He wanted them to know that when they consecrated themselves, obeyed Him, and trusted in His work, He would use them and what they had to manifest His glory. Oh what glory this is! He always desired that His people would join themselves to Him.

When He had to go to Jerusalem, He could have created a colt with His creative power in the same way that He created many animals when He furnished the earth. Yet He was happy to have the disciples go and fetch it for Him. He even said that "the Lord has need of them" (Matt. 21:3), which can be translated as "the Lord lacks them" or "the Lord is in need of them." Did the Creator really have any lack? Did He really have any need? But He said this Himself. He knew beforehand that there was a donkey with a colt tied beside her in the next village. He also knew that no man had ever sat on the colt. And He knew that the owner would question the disciples when they unloosened the colt and what they should say in order for the owner to release it to them. This was a miracle. But His condescension lies in the fact that He was happy to perform this type of miracle rather than set aside the existing colt or the disciples' errands by performing a miracle of creating a colt. He could have created a colt a hundred times better than any other colt with one word. Yet, and I say this most reverently, He was pleased to be helped by men. He was happy to see other men making contributions to His earthly journey. He was happy to have men as His companions. He was willing to receive something from His loved ones to help Him in His work. He could go on alone with no need of men. Yet He did not want to do this. He wanted to condescend a little and receive men's consecration. He wanted to elevate men and give them a part in God's work.

He said, "I have need of them," "I lack them." It seems that He was saying that His lack would not have been met if the owner of the colt had refused to give it to Him. He had a need, and He desired to see men fulfill this need. He would rather receive what He needed from the hands of His people than through His own miracle. If His people would be faithful to give, He would ride on their colt and enter Jerusalem to receive men's Hosannas. If the believers were lazy or held back, He would rather wait and allow His need to go unanswered. He was not willing to exercise His divine power to work alone. He was not in haste. This is His will; He wants to do things this way. We do not know why, but we know that this is what He wants to do. All those who understand the Lord's heart should find their own responsibility in this matter.

On the one hand, the Lord condescends. On the other hand, He elevates us. Are we worthy of such elevation? If the creatures are not elevated through the opportunity to take care of the Creator's need, what else could this be? When we consider this, we should murmur less when the Holy Spirit prompts us to consecrate. It is an absolute mistake to think that when we offer ourselves and what we have to God that we are doing God a favor or earning credits from God. Our consecration and God's acceptance of our consecration is God's elevating and bestowing His glory on us. He is the Most High God. All the angels in heaven are His servants. All the cattle and goats on the hills are His. He owns all the gold and silver on earth and thousands of worlds are His. Does He have any lack? Does He need the power and material supply of humble and poor people? Is He really helpless and seeking our help? Or is He elevating and uplifting us through these needs and making us realize that humble, lowly, poor, and destitute men such as ourselves can be counted worthy of supplying God's needs and becoming His help? This is indeed too wonderful!

Is it not a wonder that God wants our strength and material supply? Is it not a wonder that a king would want the possessions of a beggar? Is there no one who can supply Him other than beggars? Or does He have other intentions in mind? Should a beggar who is given the privilege of helping his king feel flattered or self-accomplished? Offering to our King is our extraordinary privilege.

The believers should consider what sacrifice there can be for little creatures such as we to offer anything to God. It is our privilege and special right to be able to do this. His willingness to accept our offering is sufficient honor for us. His asking of us is a far higher honor. Because our hearts are too dull and ignorant of the honor of consecration, we boast of our suffering, sacrifice, and consecration to the Lord as if we have earned some credit from Him! Oh, how believers are unappreciative of their elevation! If the present workers of the Lord realized this fact, they would not be so timid and careful. They would not save up treasures for themselves and would not consider their offering of a little money as a favor to the Lord.

The words of Mordecai are very fitting. He told queen Esther, "For if thou altogether holdest thy peace at this time, then shall there enlargement and deliverance arise to the Jews from another place...and who knoweth whether thou art come to the kingdom for such a time as this?" (Esth. 4:14). Dear brothers and sisters, today God's people have many needs. God considers these needs as His needs. He will fill these needs. However, He does not want to deliver His people by performing miracles by Himself. He wants to use you. Are you willing? He could send messengers from heaven to sound the call and revive His people. He could perform many works of wonders and strange signs to wake up sinners. He could once again send manna from heaven to feed His servants and maids who live by Him. But if He did these things, you would lose your glory and your share in God's work. He can perform miracles and grant deliverance, but He wants to do them through you. He does not want to do them by Himself. The question is whether or not we are worthy of His elevation.

He is willing that He Himself should condescend and is happy to elevate us. He is happy for us to have a share in all His works. He is humble enough to say that He has needs so that a door will be open for us to help Him and gain His glory. If this is the case, why would we not consecrate ourselves to the Lord? Why would we not offer our riches? All those who fail to grasp the present opportunities are foolish.

In summary, God needs man in His work of saving the world. If you will not help, God will raise up others to take your place. The work of helping other believers go on needs man. If you draw back, God will raise up others to take your place. God has given you money so that you will supply the need of His work. If you fail, God will raise up others. God's needs must be met, but who will meet them? Who will step forward to preach His word, and who will fill up God's glory? If you do not step forward, do not think that God will be short of help. He will raise up others. But it will be a pity that *you* will not be able to share in the glory. "For if thou altogether holdest thy peace at this time, then shall there enlargement and deliverance arise to the Jews *from another place*" (Esth. 4:14). Therefore brothers, let "*no one* take *your* crown" (Rev. 3:11).

God's need today is greater than at any other time. He is bestowing special glory to believers of this age. He is still willing to condescend. But are there believers who are willing to marvel with gratitude for such grace from God and fulfill God's need without feeling self-satisfied because of their awareness of such a high honor?

CHAPTER TWENTY

THE TWO SIDES OF THE TRUTH— SUBJECTIVE AND OBJECTIVE

Scripture Reading: John 3:16; 14:16; 15:4-5; 14:17; 6:47; 4:14; 1 John 2:8; Phil. 1:20-21; 1 Cor. 1:30; Col. 1:27

We often speak about the matter of subjective truth and objective truth. All the truths in the New Testament are divided into these two categories, and similarly all the Old Testament truths are divided into these two categories. To make this matter clear to many of you, I would first like to explain the meaning of the words *objective* and *subjective*. The literal meanings of the Chinese words for *objective* and *subjective* are "guest's view" and "host's view." Being objective is viewing things from the position of a guest or an outsider, and being subjective is viewing things from one's self as a host. Viewing things from the position of an outsider is being objective, and viewing things from within is being subjective. Whatever occurs in others is objective; whatever occurs in me is subjective. All the truths that are not in me are objective truths; all the truths that are inside of me are subjective truths. All the truths outside of me are objective truths; they are truths, even though they are outside of me. All the experiences within me are subjective and are also truths. The Bible places equal weight on both aspects of these truths. I would now like to give you some illustrations.

John 3:16 says, "For God so loved the world that He gave His only begotten Son." John 14:16 says, "And I will ask the Father, and He will give you another Comforter." It is sad that many who can recite John 3:16 so well cannot recite John 14:16. Actually these two verses are of equal worth. God had two "givings." In John 3:16 He gave His Son to us, and in John

14:16 He gave the Holy Spirit to us. God gave His Son to sinners, and He gave the Holy Spirit to the ones who believe in His Son. God gave His Son to the world that they may be saved through Him. God gave the Holy Spirit to those who believe in His Son that they may be empowered to overcome. One is the giving of the Son, and the other is the giving of the Holy Spirit. Everything accomplished in the Son is an objective truth, and everything done in us through the working of the Holy Spirit is a subjective truth. Everything that is done in Christ is objective, while everything that is done in us through the Holy Spirit is subjective. When the Lord was crucified on the cross, we were crucified there with Him. This is an objective fact. If we search within ourselves to see whether we have died, we surely will not feel that we have died. Likewise, if we preach the gospel to a sinner, telling him that he is a sinner and Christ has died for him, will he realize he has died with Christ? No matter that is in Christ is subjective. Everything in Christ is objective, and all the work done by the Holy Spirit in us is subjective. The Holy Spirit does not work in Himself; all the work of the Holy Spirit is done within us. What Christ has accomplished is in Himself, and what the Holy Spirit has accomplished is in us. As long as something or some work is done in Christ, it is objective; as long as something is accomplished by the Holy Spirit, it is subjective. Please remember this point: objective matters are in Christ, and subjective matters are within us.

In John 15:4 the Lord repeated the phrase *abide in Me* twice. What is it to "abide in Me"? It is just to abide in the Lord. Abiding in the Lord is objective. We must first have the objective aspect before we can have the experience of "I [abide] in you," which is the subjective aspect. We must remember that the words "I [abide] in you" are preceded by the words "Abide in Me." Every subjective experience is based on an objective fact. No one could ever be saved if there was just the working of the Holy Spirit without the accomplishment of Christ. Neither could people be saved by only having the accomplishment of Christ without the working of the Holy Spirit. As I have said before, a man must have two feet to stand firm and two eyes to see clearly. Birds must have two wings to fly. Similarly, we must first be in the Lord, and then He will be in us.

John 6:47 says, "He who believes has eternal life." Every believer knows this verse. It is true that we have believed, and it is true that he who believes has eternal life. However, no one can locate the eternal life. What does John 4:14 tell us? It says, "But whoever drinks of the water that I will give him shall by no means thirst forever; but the water that I will give him will become in him a spring of water gushing up into eternal life." The water that He will give us is the water of life, and it will well up from within again and again until we sense its flavor. On the one hand, the Lord talks about the eternal life, and on the other hand, He talks about a well of living water springing up which enables us to taste the flavor of eternal life. John 6:47 speaks of the objective aspect, and John 4:14 speaks of the subjective aspect. First John 2:8 says, "...which is true in Him and in you." Some of the truths are in Him, and some of the truths are in us. They are all truths, and we should pay attention to all of them. John 15 tells us how to bear fruit: "He who abides in Me and I in him, he bears much fruit" (v. 5). In other words, whenever the objective truth is balanced by the subjective truth, there will be much fruit-bearing. John 14:17 says, "The Spirit of reality...because He abides with you and shall be in you." *He abides with you* is objective. This phrase points out the fact that the Holy Spirit through Christ was with the disciples. The phrase *shall be in you* is subjective. It points to the fact of Christ dwelling in the disciples through the Holy Spirit. At one time this word was objective and outside of them, but once the Holy Spirit came and dwelt in them, the objective facts became their subjective experience.

On one hand, Paul in 1 Corinthians 1:30 said, "But of Him you are in Christ Jesus." On the other hand, in Colossians 1:27 Paul said, "Christ in you, the hope of glory." To be in Christ is the objective aspect, and to have Christ in us is the subjective aspect.

If we want to discover these two aspects of the truth in the Bible, we can find several hundred verses which show the subjective aspect of the truth as well as the objective aspect of the truth. If we can grasp these two aspects, we are able to grasp the tracks in the Bible. A train has two tracks on which to run. If there is only one track, the train will derail. With two tracks, the train can move ahead. Both the objective and subjective aspects of the truth need our attention. Emphasizing each aspect equally will render us the greatest help. I do not want to preach any theology here. Rather, I would like to speak a little on the practical side. For the time being, I will briefly mention the major accomplishments of Christ on the objective side as well as the work of the Holy Spirit on the subjective side.

First of all, Christ's death on the cross for our sins and for us is the kernel of the objective truths in the Bible. When a person touches the Bible, he will see Christ's death, Christ's redemption, and how Christ was made a propitiatory sacrifice for our sins. Once you open the Bible, you will see these things, unless you do not read it at all. He hung on the tree to personally bear our sins. This matter was accomplished on the cross. He has borne your sins, my sins, and the sins of so many people. These are the facts.

If the Lord Jesus has borne your sins, my sins, and the sins of all the people in the world, then why are all the people not saved? Why is it that some of the ones who have believed in the Lord and who we know are saved do not have the joy of salvation? Why are they grieved over their sins? They are grieved because they always see the subjective side of how inwardly sinful, filthy, and unclean they still are. Consequently, they do not see how they can be saved. We need to know that all that Christ has accomplished is on the objective side and cannot be found on the subjective side. If a lamp is on this side, how can you find it on the other side? What the Lord accomplished at Golgotha was not accomplished in us. If we search within ourselves, we will never find it. Although I cannot find Christ's dying for us within, can it be found on the cross? If Christ's death for us can be found on the cross, then we can declare, "Hallelujah! Christ has borne my sins; I am saved." Whenever our faith latches on to the objective things, the Holy Spirit will infuse power into our inner being and will cause us to have the peace of forgiveness and the joy of salvation. If we try to find the death of Christ on the subjective side, we will never be able to find it because this is not God's way. God first gave His Son to man, and then He gave the Holy Spirit to man. The giving of the Holy Spirit follows the giving of God's Son. Christ came first, then the Holy Spirit. What the Holy Spirit is doing is to complete in us what the Lord has accomplished on His side.

The book of Hebrews tells us that faith is like an anchor, secure and firm, which brings us within the veil (Heb. 6:19). Suppose we are on a ship with a very large anchor. If it is always kept on the ship, what use is this anchor? The anchor should be cast into the water to keep the ship from rocking; it should not be kept on the ship. This is how faith should operate. Faith never comes from believing in ourselves; faith comes from casting our anchor in the Lord Jesus, casting from our side to His side. Whenever something on the objective side is grasped by us, the subjective side becomes secure in us. Suppose a ship with an anchor on board is rocking incessantly. Will fastening and putting more anchors on the ship cause it to steady? Even if the ship had larger anchors or was filled with anchors, it would still rock unsteadily. The ship will only become steady when the anchor is cast into the water. The more we look at ourselves, the more disappointed we will become. If we cast our faith upon the cross of the Lord Jesus, we will be at peace. We must be secure on the other side before we can be secure on our side; the order cannot be reversed. The correct way is to take the objective aspect as the starting point and then have the subjective aspect as the issue. If we only emphasize Christ's accomplishment on the cross without caring for what the Holy Spirit wants to do in us, we will never be able to have the experience. Similarly, if we only emphasize the Holy Spirit within us without caring for Christ's accomplishment on the cross, the result will be futile.

For example, in the matter of being crucified with Christ, is it we who crucify ourselves? No. Romans 6:6 tells us, "Knowing this, that our old man has been crucified with Him in order that the body of sin might be annulled, that we should no longer serve sin as slaves." We do not do the crucifying; our old man was crucified with Christ when He was

crucified on the cross. This is an objective truth. Our
eyes must be on the Lord. It would be terrible if we were to
crucify ourselves. Even though we see our wretchedness, we
are not able to crucify it. The biggest mistake believers make
is to say, "Even though the Bible says I have died with Christ,
when I look at myself, I realize that I am still so hard-hearted.
It is very easy for me to lose my temper; I am still so bad and
not good." We are crucified with Him, but the more we try,
the less we die. We are wrong because we are starting from
our end. We should remember that Christ is the real beginning to everything. The real death is not seeing ourselves
dead; when Christ died, we also died with Him. Only when
the anchor is cast is it effectual. Faith is efficacious only
when it is cast in Christ. If our eyes are always on ourselves,
we cannot be crucified. Our pretense to be dead is a fake
death, and we have no way to put ourselves to death. We have
already died with Christ on the cross; this was accomplished
by Christ. On the objective side Christ has died, and we have
also died.

Romans 8:13 says, "For if you live according to the flesh,
you must die, but if by the Spirit you put to death the practices of the body, you will live." This verse runs parallel to
Romans 6:6, which speaks of being crucified with Christ; this
verse speaks of putting to death the practices of the body by
the Spirit. Crucifixion was accomplished by Christ, whereas
the putting to death is done by the Spirit. I believe that I have
been crucified with Christ. For this I can say, "Hallelujah!"
When Christ died, my old man was crucified with Him. Today,
on the subjective side, the Spirit will bring up a matter and
tell you that this matter has been crucified on the cross. Will
you follow the speaking of the Spirit? If you say you are
willing, the matter will be dealt with. Then the next day the
Spirit will bring up another matter and tell you that it has
been crucified on the cross. Are you willing to go along with
His speaking? If you agree, another matter will be dealt with.
The Spirit will say, "Your temper has been crucified on the
cross. You do not need to lose your temper." If you say, "I am
willing not to lose my temper," then the Spirit will give you
the power not to lose your temper. The Spirit will then say

that your pride has been crucified and that you can be freed from your pride. If you agree with not being proud, the Spirit will give you the power not to be proud. If you are willing to go along with the Spirit in one matter after another, the Spirit will fulfill His work in you. If you only depend on yourself to suppress your anger, you will find that even gritting your teeth will not work. You must first see the accomplishment of Christ's death on the objective side before the Spirit will carry out that death in you.

In the first two centuries, believers greeted each other by saying, "The Lord is coming soon," or, "In Christ." Indeed, once we see that we are in Christ, everything is sweet and precious. At the same time, the Spirit within us will put to death the deeds of the body. Today Christians pay too much attention to either the objective truth or the subjective truth. When one pays too much attention to the subjective truth, he suppresses himself. This is like an anchor that is not cast into the water; it is useless. Then there are others who think that because Christ has died, they do not need to care for anything. This is also wrong. Christ has indeed died on the cross; but if you do not believe this, you will still perish. However, if you believe that Christ has died on the cross and are willing to believe in Him, you will be saved. Likewise, when the Spirit says to you that your temper, pride, and jealousy have been crucified, if you are willing and have the desire, the Spirit will give you the power to overcome. When you believe the objective truth, the Spirit will simultaneously make the objective truth your subjective experience. The Spirit will fulfill the outward truth you believe in you. The Spirit will fulfill what you believe has been accomplished on the cross in you.

This is not only the case with the truth of our death with Christ, but it also applies to the truth of resurrection. Ephesians 2:6 says, "And raised us up together...in Christ Jesus." How are we resurrected? We are resurrected with Him. This is of Christ and is an objective truth. Resurrection is not only spoken of in Ephesians; Peter also said, "God...has regenerated us unto a living hope through the resurrection of Jesus Christ from the dead" (1 Pet. 1:3). In other words, the time when a Christian is regenerated is the time when he is resurrected together with Christ. Actually, every regenerated Christian has been resurrected with the Lord, and every Christian who has been resurrected with the Lord has been regenerated. We have been resurrected with Him, and He has raised us up.

What is the meaning of resurrection? The Lord Jesus died in His body; all the blood in His body was shed; He suffered numerous wounds on His head from the crown of thorns; He had wounds on His hands and feet and a gash on His side from a spear. This is the power of death that took hold of His body. When God's life came into His body, He became alive. This is the meaning of resurrection. This life overcame all the effects of death in His body; it healed all the wounds and did away with all the pain. This is resurrection. Formerly, the eyes could not see, the ears could not hear, and the hands could not move; now they are all able to function. To be dead, according to the Bible, is to be absolutely powerless and utterly weak. Death is spiritual inability and impossibility. Formerly, the Lord was bound by numerous burial cloths. But what happened at the time of resurrection? The resurrection of the Lord was vastly different from that of Lazarus. When Lazarus came out of the tomb, his hands and feet were bound with cloth, and his face was bound with a handkerchief. He needed someone else to set him free. On the contrary, regarding the Lord's resurrection, the Bible says, "He beheld the linen cloths lying there and the handkerchief which had been over His head, not lying with the linen cloths, but folded up in one place apart" (John 20:6-7). The Lord did not slowly cut His cloths loose. God's power and life entered in and loosened every lawful or unlawful bondage. What was a corpse became a moving and liberated being. This was the resurrection of the Lord.

I remember, when I first began to work for the Lord, I would ask the Lord to resurrect me together with Him. I thought that if the Lord would resurrect me together with Him, then I would have the power to do God's will. I was wrong in praying that way because it was something initiated by me. The Bible says I have been resurrected together with

Christ. This is an accomplished fact. Please remember that the more we turn to ourselves, the worse we will be. It is not that we should not have subjective experiences, but we should first believe the objective truth. I can now say, "Lord, I thank You; You have resurrected, and I have been resurrected together with You." We must first believe the fact that we have been resurrected. How were we resurrected? Do we feel like we have resurrected? No, it is Christ who resurrected us. We can ask how we were saved. While we were yet sinners, we heard the gospel that the Lord Jesus died for us and cleansed us from our sins with His blood. We believed and were immediately saved. We did not look at ourselves to see whether we were qualified, but we looked away to what the Lord accomplished on the cross. Once we lay hold of this fact, we will be at peace.

However, if we only pay attention to the objective truth and not to the subjective truth, we are like one-winged birds trying to fly. We should not emphasize one half and neglect the other. Ephesians 2:6 tells us that we have been raised up together with Christ Jesus. On the other hand, Ephesians 1:19-20 says, "And what is the surpassing greatness of His power toward us who believe, according to the operation of the might of His strength, which He caused to operate in Christ." Although the believers in Ephesus were resurrected with Christ, the apostle Paul still wanted them to know the exceeding greatness of His power. Verse 19 tells us the greatness of this power; verse 20 tells us that this power is the resurrection power. In other words, although we have been resurrected, we still need to know the greatness of this power. On the objective side we have resurrection; on the subjective side we still need to know the power of resurrection. One cannot say, "My temper has been crucified, but I still can lose my temper." On the objective side his temper has been crucified, but on the subjective side he should still put his temper to death by the Spirit. On the subjective side he still needs to be empowered by the Spirit to deny the world and obey God's will. With the reality of the objective aspect, one still needs to have the subjective experiences. One very bad phenomenon is that some people do not believe the objective facts but only focus their efforts on subjective experiences. Other people only believe the objective facts and ignore the subjective experiences. According to the Bible, if one lacks faith, he will never experience spiritual deliverance, and if he lacks obedience, he will also not experience spiritual deliverance. Faith is toward what Christ has accomplished, while obedience is specifically toward what the Spirit will accomplish. Faith is toward Christ, and obedience is toward the Spirit. Therefore, it is very crucial to believe and obey.

Philippians 3:10 says, "To know Him and the power of His resurrection." Paul said that the goal of his counting all things loss was to know the power of resurrection. He did not say he wanted to know resurrection, because once a person has believed, he has resurrection. But on the subjective side he still needed to count all things loss in order to know the power of His resurrection.

Ascension is the last great accomplished truth in the New Testament. The Lord's incarnation, crucifixion, resurrection and ascension are some of the greatest truths in the Bible. Concerning the Lord's ascension, you do not know how much time I spent shortly after I was saved thinking how good it would be if only I could daily sit in the heavenlies and have my sin under my feet. I was like an airplane in the sky that could not stay in the sky forever. I continually besought the Lord that one day I would be able to sit steadily in the heavenlies and break my record of ascension. Then one day I read Ephesians 2:6: "And raised us up together with Him and seated us together with Him in the heavenlies in Christ Jesus." I realized then that when Christians were raised up together with Christ, they were also seated together with Him in the heavenlies. This is not due to their diligence or prayers. It is because Christ brought us into the heavenlies when He ascended. Because He is in the heavenlies, I am also in the heavenlies. However, I should allow the power of the Lord's ascension to be manifested in me.

On the other hand, Colossians 3:1-3 says, "If therefore you were raised together with Christ, seek the things which are above, where Christ is, sitting at the right hand of God. Set your mind on the things which are above, not on the things which are on the earth. For you died, and your life is hidden with Christ in God." This is subjective. Ascension means that our life has been hidden with Christ in God. Because we have died, resurrected, and ascended, we ought to seek the things which are above and daily set our mind on the things which are above. Suppose a sinner hears that the Lord Jesus has died for him and thinks that since the Lord has died for him, he can go on sinning. We all know that this is not right. We have the position of ascension. However, if we continually set our mind on the things that are on the earth, even our ascended position will do us no good. If we believe in Christ's ascension and, at the same time, continually set our minds on the things above rather than the things on earth, we will not only be in the heavenlies objectively, but we will also be in the heavenlies subjectively.

Brothers, only having objective facts without having subjective experience is too theoretical; one will not have any taste of heaven from this. It is absolutely necessary to believe all that Christ has done on the objective side. It is also absolutely necessary to obey what the Spirit wants to do on the subjective side. All spiritual experiences come first from believing what Christ has accomplished and then by obeying the Spirit's leading. Christ's accomplishments cause us to gain the position; the Spirit's leading causes us to gain the experiences. The accomplishments of Christ are facts for us to believe. The leading of the Spirit is the principle for us to obey. All spiritual experiences begin from the objective side; there is no exception. Our anchor must be cast in Christ's death, resurrection, and ascension.

John 15:4-5 says, "Abide in Me and I in you. As the branch cannot bear fruit of itself unless it abides in the vine, so neither can you unless you abide in Me. I am the vine; you are the branches. He who abides in Me and I in him, he bears much fruit; for apart from Me you can do nothing." The order in this passage is most important. Being "in Me" is first. The "Me" in this verse is the Lord. One must first be in Christ. This is the objective side. Then "I in you" follows. "I in you" is Christ abiding in us. This is the subjective side. We must first have the objective aspect; then the subjective aspect will be added. What follows thereafter is a promise that we will bear much fruit. Being in the Lord is the objective side. Once we have the objective side, then we will have the subjective side of the Lord abiding in us. When we believe in the objective fact, everything on the objective side will come into us. The issue of the objective plus the subjective is fruit-bearing. There will not be any fruit-bearing if we only have the objective side; similarly, we will not bear any fruit if we just have the subjective side. Whenever the objective and subjective sides are joined together, there will be fruit-bearing.

When the church began in Jerusalem, there were both men and women praying in the upper room. In typology, men represent the objective truth, while women represent the subjective truth. The presence of men typifies the presence of objective truth or doctrine, while the presence of women typifies the presence of subjective truth or experience. The result of this was three thousand and then five thousand souls being saved. This was the way the church began. In the future, at the time of Christ's second coming, there will be the Lamb of God on the objective side. There will also be the bride of the Lamb, "clothed in fine linen, bright and clean; for the fine linen is the righteousnesses of the saints" (Rev. 19:8). This is the subjective aspect.

Whether or not the Lord is pleased with a Christian's living depends on how balanced he is regarding these two aspects. In the church today, some preach only the subjective truth. An example of this is the so-called holiness group; they only have the female aspect. However, others only teach the objective truth. An example of this is the Brethren; they only have the male aspect. Both of these extremes suffer loss. By paying attention only to the subjective side, one not only fails to gain any experience, but he also suffers daily. On the other hand, those who pay attention solely to the objective side and live a carefree daily life, thinking that they have died, resurrected, and ascended with Christ and, therefore, need not care for anything else, will not have any experience either. God's way is not to pay attention only to the objective side or only to the subjective side. The principle in the Bible is for us to first have the objective aspect and then the subjective aspect. We should first have the facts of Christ and then follow the leading of the Holy Spirit. The result will be much fruit-bearing. May God teach us to obey Him more and serve Him more according to His way.

5/29/2023 The Privilege of God's
Children (Matt 7:7-11

1) God's Property – right to the inheritance – Heirs of God
2) Indwelt by the Holy Spirit
3) Joint heirs with Christ
4) Have power of attorney
5) Answers to prayer

— Romans 9:4-5

OTHER BOOKS PUBLISHED BY
Living Stream Ministry

Titles by Witness Lee:

Titles by Watchman Nee:

Available at
Christian bookstores, or contact Living Stream Ministry
2431 W. La Palma Ave. • Anaheim, CA 92801
1-800-549-5164 • www.livingstream.com